"*I want this book to inform you and cause you to think about your own life. I hope that my story brings you to reflect deeply on your purpose and direction.*

Perhaps you are doing precisely what you want, and everything is exactly as you wish it to be. Maybe not. If not, like me, you never know when death will come knocking, and it's your time to move on."

Kellan Fluckiger

Meeting God at the Door

Meeting God at the Door
Conversations, Choices, and Commitments of a Near Death Experience

Kellan Fluckiger

RED AUSSIE
— PUBLISHING —

Meeting God at the Door

Conversations, Choices and Commitments of a Near Death Experience
Copyright © 2018 by Kellan Fluckiger

Published in Phoenix, Arizona, by Red Aussie Publishing
22424 S Ellsworth Loop Rd
Unit 898
Queen Creek, AZ 85142

Contact the Publisher:
RedAussiePublishing@gmail.com
www.RedAussiePublishing.com

Contact the author:
www.KellanFluckiger.com

ISBN: 978-1-7328588-2-4
Cover Design by Joy Fluckiger
Interior Design by Joy Fluckiger

Table of Contents

Foreword

A few days ago, I received a text from Kellan Fluckiger. My 'Mission' should I choose to accept it, was an invitation to write the Foreword for the first of his two newest books, Meeting God at the Door.

Why me? I can't say for sure, but I can tell you in my own words who Kellan is in my life and why it's not all that unusual for me to get texts from him which challenge me in yet another new way.

Kellan is 'Uncle Kellan' around here, though we're not related, as I don't have any 'real' Uncles. He would probably say he's my Coach or Mentor. I've been a client of his coaching practice for several years now. We speak about once a week, and every so often I go stay with him and Joy for a couple of days of intense work on myself.

I could tell you about his resume, but I'm sure there is some Bio which has that handled. Besides, if you're like me, those things don't impress much anymore, so I'll spare both of us. Kellan is a special vessel of intensity on fire with twin turbos like I've not met before.

There are many stories but, just, for example, he once disrupted a congressional committee meeting with the intensive energy of his listening. Yes, listening. He's just like that, all the time.

He's seen and done things that I've not done, high highs and low lows and through his unique Kellan-ness, he's served me in this special 'Uncle Kellan' role, which has rescued me from 40 years of tortured thinking about my own flaws and short-comings.

He's dragged me, often kicking and screaming, due to my addiction to self-pity, from hopeless to hopeful, broken to fruitful, and sadness to grateful. From the outside, no normal people were able to see my *Dead Man Walking* existence. He saw right through it and demanded that I take control of it before it was too late. My wife and I are very grateful for Kellan!

Recently, as you will read, Kellan took his unique Kellan-ness to another level by almost dying. Using his prolific intellect and creativity to capture the raw details and amazing emotional impacts of his near-death conversations with God, he is sharing those experiences with the rest of us through two new books.

Back to my 'Mission.' How easy would it have been to believe that I did not have time to write such an important thing? How common would it be for me to believe that I don't have the skill or the talent to write the Foreword to such an important book?

How easy to feel unworthy of the Mission or to believe that it must be the job of someone else who is more this or more that? I just introduced you to the energy of Kellan, how logical would it seem for me to believe that I don't possess the energy or power to hold up to the task asked of me?

Wouldn't any of those beliefs be perfectly normal?

Wouldn't it also be perfectly normal to worry about all those inadequacies until the window of time for this mission had passed so that I miss the opportunity to give my best effort? And once I miss it, to lament that failure for the rest of my days? I could easily add it to that giant pile of failures in the back of my mind.

But it didn't have to go that way; I can choose to believe an entirely different reality for myself and I can choose to engage in an entirely different set of actions. I can create for myself, my 'Uncle,' and my God an entirely new outcome with *this* Mission and countless more to come through all the remaining days of life I'm gifted with.

Please choose to allow yourself however many minutes you require to consume this book and the *Book of Context* to follow. Just choose to. If you're not a 'good reader' that's okay, forgive yourself and choose to believe you'll get through it. Then do so.

You probably don't know Kellan as I do, but that's okay too. Open your heart and 'listen' to his story with love and no judgment. Choose to receive the good news of your status in the eyes of God as it was explained to Kellan at the doorway. Choose to believe that you are full enough to fulfill your own Mission.

Thanks for sharing this time with me, I can't wait to hear what you choose to believe.

Thank you, Kellan, for this Mission. Thank you, Kellan, for this book. Thank you, Kellan, for being the best Kellan you can be. May God bless your Mission, however many you may reach along the way.

Shawn Miller

Holland, Michigan

August 2018

"We are here for a purpose.

We are here to discover, develop and deliver our divine gifts and talents, and to decide whether or not we want to Add Good to the World'.

Kellan Fluckiger

Introduction

When I was 10 or 11, I overheard my parents talking about a fellow named Charlie. He was a rowdy guy; the town "bad boy." He had "died," then had a conversation with someone on the other side. He had a choice about whether to come back to live a better life or to pass on to the next place. He chose to return.

I didn't know about all that, but after that happened, Charlie was a completely different person. I understand now that such change is quite common. Many military personnel who endure such an experience are entirely transformed and have no more desire to be "tough guys."

An acclaimed neurologist, who for all his professional career maintained that such experiences are created in our minds and that there was no afterlife, experienced this for himself. Afterward, his view changed completely, and he wrote a book about his transformation.

I guess it makes sense that a broader vision of who we are, what we're doing here, and the context of future certainly has the potential to change radically one's view about what is and isn't the kind of legacy one wants to create.

In the past few years, I've read some articles and a few books about these experiences. I've certainly noted the striking similarity that seems to be present.

There is generally some description of "going into the light." There is always a description of some peaceful feeling, and quite often, the issue of choice comes up. Specifically, whether the dying person wants to move on or return and have more time on earth.

I might have been inclined to think that you always would opt for more time since moving on is moving into the unknown, which can always be frightening. However, given the description of the peaceful circumstance, many opt to go on whose stories we never hear.

I was raised in a religious home, overly vigilant and physically abusive. The abuse was tied to forcing me into doing the things that were "good," so I would be "saved," later.

Such circumstances often drive people away from God, religion, or even spirituality altogether. It was not so with me. I knew there was something beyond this life, and I always had a yearning to understand the bigger picture.

As I work today as a coach and mentor for individuals who are driven to accomplish greater things, I notice the vast majority of these clients also have a deep knowledge that there is more. Sometimes I'm the first person they talk to about these yearnings; a safe place where they feel like they can explore true feelings.

I'm not saying that everyone who wants to be a high achiever has to be religious or spiritual. I am saying that I see it as a common characteristic, and I find it striking that such a universal yearning exists.

Some people brush it off as a need for structure or a need for some higher power outside ourselves. There have been enough examples of these near-death experiences and the mighty change that comes afterward, to eliminate that opinion as an expression of fear or trying to hide from the unknown. This is akin to when people still wanted to believe the earth was flat.

Having said all that, if you read my book, *Tightrope of Depression*, you know that I've had other experiences from outside of this reality.

Divine intervention is what shook me out of my addiction and set me on the path to recovery. However, that intervention was one-way and didn't involve a conversation, bright lights or anything of the sort. It was simply a statement that I interpreted as an opportunity to change.

If you want details, you can read that book and get familiar with what happened in my life from very young up through age 52, which is when that first event occurred.

I already knew that there are powers beyond our understanding, but I didn't know how specifically focused and powerful they can be on each of us individually.

In the ten years between that event and today, I've pursued every possible means to understand how we connect and relate to the larger universe, to the unknown, to the divine.

I've come to know, without question, that there are massive powers and purposes beyond our understanding that are available to us, structured for our good and our opportunity.

The bottom line is that we are here for a purpose. We are here to discover, develop and deliver our divine gifts and talents, and to decide whether or not we want to "Add Good to the World."

I fully realize that everyone has their own story, mythology, and beliefs surrounding the meaning of this life and whether there is life after we pass and the meaning of such a new existence.

I'm not writing this book to convince anyone of any particular viewpoint, especially since you can't convince anyone of anything. Change is a choice that comes from within. I'm certainly not writing just to add to the pile of books that describe similar experiences.

I'm writing this book for three reasons:

1. I need to write about it. I feel compelled to report what happened as I lay dying in the intensive care ward at the University of Alberta Hospital after having been struck with antibiotic-resistant pneumonia in both lungs (necrotizing MRSA). I must add my voice to all those others who describe such an experience and contribute to the body of evidence that life has a purpose and infinite opportunity.

2. I want to share a powerful guiding principle, which is: God is available to every one of us. He is not some distant mystical figure that peeks over at the earth once in a while. He is personal, pays attention to everything we do, and walks the delicate balance between never interfering with our freedom to choose and the great desire of a loving parent to give his children every opportunity.

3. I have a mission. I must let every person I can know the truth of their divine origin, infinite potential and the availability of all the help they need to develop to their fullest capability. The second part of the mission is to help as many people as I can discover, develop and deliver their own divine gifts in the service of others.

I'm not writing this book to create a following, or make predictions about the future, or explain how the afterlife works, or drive anyone to adopt my views or join some church.

I've seen dozens of books where people describe near-death experiences. Some have outlandish claims of knowledge and prophecy and seem more interested in creating a splash than sharing a compelling experience.

I want none of that. I wasn't even going to write this, but the experience wouldn't leave me alone. I had the distinct impression, as part of the deal I made, that the story needed to be told and that I, needed to describe what happened.

So here it is.

I want this book to inform you and cause you to think about your own life. I hope that my story brings you to reflect deeply on your purpose and direction.

Perhaps you're doing precisely what you want, and everything is exactly as you wish it to be. Maybe not. If not, like me, you never know when death will come knocking, and it's your time to move on.

This stark reality has caused me great excitement and focus as I think about the future.

Prologue

I sat in the emergency room at the University of Alberta Hospital in Edmonton, Alberta, Canada. It was about 11 am on June 8, 2018, and my biggest concern at this moment was breathing.

I expected to be there two or three hours before it was my turn. If you have been to the emergency room, you know the drill. You sit for a couple of hours, they call you into a semi-private piece of the ER where the beds are separated only by thin curtains on ceiling tracks.

Then you wait for a while on an uncomfortable bed until finally, the overworked medical staff finds the time to come and see what's wrong.

I was trying not to cough too much, so I didn't freak out all the people sitting around me. When I did cough, I was bringing up foul colored phlegm that was scary looking.

Suddenly I heard my name called. I looked up in disbelief. It had only been about 10 minutes, and I couldn't believe that they were calling me ahead of all these people that had been there longer.

I followed the nurse, showing me to a private room. This room had a door and was completely isolated. I didn't even know they *had* those rooms in the ER.

The nurse took my vital signs, listened to my lungs and did all the standard tests. Then she asked what I was feeling and why I had come to the ER. I told her this was my fifth day of this illness. It had started on Monday and gotten worse every day since.

The last couple of days had been exponentially worse, and that decline had been what finally convinced me to go to the doctor instead of trying to get better on my own.

I told her we had been on vacation to Europe, that I had first felt bad on Monday in Oslo, Norway. Our trip ended on Tuesday, and I had been in Edmonton since late Tuesday afternoon.

Since returning, I had spent most of the time in bed but had still not understood how bad this was going to get. The nurse took some notes and told me the doctor would be in to see me shortly.

I lay there waiting, expecting again to pass an hour or two until the doctor got to me in due course. Once more, I was blown away when it was less than 10 minutes before the doctor came in.

He asked me where I had been to Europe and some details about the trip. I told him we had been on an eight-day cruise of the Baltic Sea and gave him a list of the cities we visited.

He pressed for more details about when I started feeling sick and precisely what the symptoms were. We talked a few more minutes, and he said he would come back in a little bit.

In 15 or 20 minutes he was back. I was amazed at the speed with which they were handling me and started to wonder what that meant.

He told me that at a minimum, I had severe pneumonia in both lungs. They were going to admit me in the hospital just as fast as they could find a bed available in the general hospital ward.

He said he suspected what I had was much worse than just pneumonia and mentioned that I might need to go to the intensive care unit.

I was left alone for a couple of hours as they looked for a place to put me. Eventually, the nurse returned with some help and announced that I was going to the fifth floor. They had found a room.

On the fifth floor, I was moved into a regular bed. Once again, they took all the medical measurements, and I was left alone.

Sensing now that this might be serious, I began to meditate, which is a tool I have used for 45 years, to go inside my body and see what I could feel. In the stillness inside, I knew something was seriously wrong.

The doctor returned and told me that they were going to move me to intensive care. Then he asked me a question that froze the blood in my veins.

"Do we have permission to do anything we need, including intubation, a to preserve your life?" The implications of that question scared me. "Yes," I whispered.

At that time, neither one of us could have known that the bug which infected me has a 10-day kill rate of 100% if not quickly identified and aggressively treated. Then the kill rate drops to a mere 60%.

Five days were already gone.

Part I – Countdown to Death

Chapter 1

Day 1 – Oslo, Norway

Oslo, like many European cities, is built around the central train station. Joy had found us a cool hotel downtown called the "City Box." The place was a bit of a cross between a regular hotel and a hostel.

The reception desk was replaced by futuristic kiosks to handle everything. One employee sat in a room off to the side behind a computer, likely to handle unusual or difficult situations. Our check-in and stay were uneventful and without interaction. The rooms were small and really only made for sleeping, showering and getting ready for the day.

The main floor common area included a kitchen with appliances, a large sectional and television, a library and other spaces just for socializing. It also looked like it was used for business meetings, as there were conference rooms of three different sizes. Quite an innovative approach to space in the central city.

We had just finished our eight-day cruise around the Baltic Sea. Before we made this amazing trip, I had never been on a cruise, and I was only vaguely aware where the Baltic Sea was located.

It was fun and interesting to learn things like that the Baltic Sea runs mostly East and West and that most of the cities we visited, Stockholm, Helsinki, St. Petersburg and Tallinn are all on about the same latitude and north of Edmonton.

It let me put some geography around many of the former Soviet states and gave me a much more connected feel to that part of the world. Sometimes I think we are all a little bit too isolated and don't really have a sense of what goes on around us.

My wife, on the other hand, is a seasoned traveler and had been all over Europe many times in previous years and was excited to go once again.

However, like me, she had never been on a cruise. So, when the opportunity came for us to grab this eight-day jaunt to several cities in this region, she jumped on it, and I went along for the ride.

Since we were right downtown, we spent our first day in the city wandering up and down the main shopping street. It was blocked off, so only foot traffic was allowed. All along both sides were eateries and shops of all kinds.

One particular street had every high-end shop I've never heard of and a few others besides. As a seasoned shopper, Joy could tell me what every store sold, what they specialized in, and where they ranked from expensive to ridiculous. We wandered around and checked out the stores and the parks.

The second day in Oslo began differently. Compared to the previous day, the humidity felt more oppressive, the distances seemed further, and I just wasn't myself. I chalked it up to our long walks in excessive heat. The local shopkeepers said that it was the hottest May-June in over 100 years. That was not what I needed.

There were museums, famous buildings and of course the royal palace on Joy's "must-see" list for the day. We mapped out a walk of several kilometers to squeeze it all in.

We had to check out of the hotel, so the first thing we did was make our way to the train station. We found a rental locker and stowed our heavy gear so that we only had the smaller backpacks to schlep.

Joy is something of an expert on European history, landmarks, and architecture, having studied Art History. She always researches the cities in advance and knows the highlights and many places off the typical tourist track.

One museum had a special exhibit, the paintings of Edvard Münch. He's the guy who painted "The Scream," where a guy is holding the side of his face, and the face is elongated, and he looks like he's uttering the primal scream from the center of the earth.

The original was on display, as well as a number of other paintings by the same artist, so there were lots of patrons in the museum that day. It's funny because Joy later read that the artist remarked "I don't know what I was thinking when I painted that, I'll never paint anything like that again."

That's interesting since it turns out to be his most famous piece of work. You never know what's going to turn out to be a big deal.

We had two places left to go. The Royal Palace and Gardens, and a skincare shop Joy had discovered. The skincare shop sells a brand she had become aware of in Australia and was excited to go. I walked up and down the street looking into other buildings while she engaged the shopkeeper and made some purchases.

Our last stop was the Royal Palace and Gardens. I learned that when the flag is up, royalty is in residence. When the flag is down, they are away somewhere. It always blows my mind to think of some person living in a place that big. There are so many rooms and so much space, on the one hand, it seems luxurious; on the other, it looks like an enormous waste of resources.

However, I wasn't there to have a political discussion; I was just there to take in the beautiful scenery and the history. It was all interesting and enjoyable except for one thing. As the early afternoon wore on, I was getting noticeably short of breath, and certainly not feeling like I expected to.

In the Royal Gardens, I had to stop and sit under a tree for 20 minutes to catch my breath. I blamed the weather, and besides, I didn't know what to do about it. I didn't understand why. I wasn't carrying any luggage. We'd already gone to the train station and put the backpacks in a locker for the day.

Fatigue finally got the better of me, and we headed straight to the train station because I just couldn't do anymore, I was feeling exhausted. We got there, we grabbed our luggage and something to eat, then boarded the train to the airport.

As we waited for our flight, we had a great conversation about how wonderful the trip had been. We'd been to many places new to both of us, seen all kinds of history and architecture, and enjoyed a delightful time together.

I was grateful to be married to such a beautiful woman, especially one who knew so much about European history and architecture and could be my personal tour guide.

Underneath all this, however, I knew that something was out of order. I was hoping that this malaise would pass quickly and wouldn't affect getting back to my clients when we got home.

At the airport, I was walking slower and slower. I just assumed it was a result of having heat exhaustion and dragging our packs around. I sucked it up and got moving with only minor complaints about how heavy the bags were.

Soon after we boarded the Norwegian air flight to Amsterdam, it was getting pretty obvious that I was distressed. The flight attendant noticed that I looked flushed and asked if I was okay.

I said, "Yes. I think I have a mild case of heat exhaustion and would appreciate some ice in a towel or water."

They were very accommodating and kept me well supplied during the flight. The towels made the temperature go down, and I wasn't moving or carrying anything, so my sense of well-being improved markedly.

We arrived in Amsterdam without incident. If you've never been there, the Schiphol Airport is enormous. It's a major European hub. It's also a self-contained city. There are stores of every kind, and you could probably live there. It wouldn't surprise me if people were doing that somewhere in the bowels of the gigantic structure.

From Amsterdam, we were going to fly to Edmonton, but that flight wasn't until 3 o'clock the next afternoon. So, we were going to spend the night at a hotel in the city center where we could while away the day.

Joy had found this amazing place through Airbnb. It was just a few hundred yards from the central train station and overlooked the Central Plaza and one of the main shopping streets, ideal for tourists.

We jumped on the train and made our way to the center of Amsterdam and the central train station. Like the airport, it's also an enormous collection of trains, buses, trams, restaurants, and every kind of shop you can imagine.

Leaving the train station schlepping all of our luggage, I began to feel as if I were sinking into the pavement. Joy assured me that our accommodations were only a few hundred yards from where we, were so I gritted my teeth and moved ahead. It seemed like 100 miles.

We must've passed 600 trams, 9 million bicycles and an uncounted number of people wandering from here to there. If you've never been to Amsterdam, you have no concept of the number of bicycles that can fit in one square mile.

I think that at least 50 to 60% of those who live in Amsterdam travel by bicycle and either do not own a car or have no need for one. There are so many bicycles that they have specific bicycle lanes and even stoplights for bikes.

For the uninitiated, that means you must watch out, or you're going to get run over by aggressive cyclists heading to or from work. More than once I jumped out of the way of a rider hustling through a yellow light. It's quite amazing.

By this time, my misery was palpable, and I knew something was up. What otherwise would have been an exciting experience turned into a painful, foggy haze.

It was already dark by the time we got to our room. The staircase was narrow and winding as you would expect in an old building. The room was well appointed and had several windows facing the vast square and the train station. The sounds from the restaurants below were jovial and loud.

Under other circumstances I would have enjoyed the revelry, but, in the present situation I tuned it all out and went to bed. I had no interest in dinner and was trying to figure out how to get to sleep as fast as possible.

The night passed in agony. At first, I couldn't fall asleep at all. I took some cold medication to try to address what I assumed were severe flu symptoms.

Eventually, fatigued overcame the churning in my body, and I slipped into a restless sleep. I had a fever that was rising quickly, and I began to sweat and toss and turn.

I didn't know how much sweat one body could produce over the course of a few hours. The bedding was soon wet enough to wring out. I got up to go to the bathroom, and when I came back, the bed was cold and entirely impossible to lie on.

Fortunately, the room was big enough for a large tourist group with four single beds and some couches. The single beds were all pushed together to make into two queen beds on opposite sides of the room. I took one, and Joy took the other, realizing that I was going to have a rough night.

On finding my first bed completely unusable, I simply moved to the other side and tried once again to get some sleep. The rest of the night was kinder to me, and I was able to doze off for a few hours.

Chapter 2

Day 2 – Amsterdam, Netherlands

Our flight the next day was at three in the afternoon, so there was no rush to get up. We didn't have a tourist agenda other than visiting one retail store which we had briefly seen when we initially landed in Amsterdam and spent the day there before the cruise started.

It turns out the store has its headquarters in Ireland, but neither Joy nor I had seen it anywhere else except there on the main shopping street. We wanted to go back just to see it one more time.

I got up late and showered and slowly dressed. We made it downstairs just in time for the breakfast buffet included with the room. It's a good thing we did because the breakfast was terrific.

It was a full spread of eggs, bacon, sausage, European pastries, and an endless list of tasty items I can't begin to remember. The sights and smells were exciting, and we lingered over breakfast until 10 o'clock before setting out for the short walk to the store we wanted to visit.

Fortunately, we were able to stow our luggage at the hotel, and I didn't have to drag it all over the place. I was extremely grateful.

It's interesting how much our mental focus amplifies some feelings and minimizes others. The increasing grip of whatever illness I had seemed to shrink as the day went on, and I instead focused on what we were going to do with the rest of our time in Amsterdam.

As we walked down the sidewalk the few blocks to the store, Joy was fascinated by the architecture. The majority of the buildings have been there for hundreds of years. It's funny in that all the lower floors are retail while the upper levels are residential.

We saw several buildings that were leaning to one side or the other. One was even leaning a bit toward the street. We also saw several buildings where the lower floor or two was occupied by a retail business and the upper floors were boarded up.

The juxtaposition of the garish modern retail, and the ancient, sometimes crumbling buildings was something to behold. I guess the builders will eventually figure out how to tear down the top half of the building and build on top of the bottom, or else they'll tear the whole thing down and start over.

In many cases, I think the only thing holding the building up is the fact that they are all right next to each other, so each neighboring buildings keep the others from falling.

Dodging another stream of bicycles, and a hoard of tourists, we made our way to the store and spent about an hour looking through things. We each found a couple of souvenirs to take home and made our last purchases.

Whatever was going on inside of me seemed to ebb and flow. Sometimes I was weak and tired, and other times things seem to be almost okay. Fortunately, this was one of the times when it backed off a little bit, so the few hours we had before our departure turned out just right.

The hotel was on our way back, so it was easy to stop and grab our luggage, stuff our purchases inside and walk to the train station.

Our train was on track 11. We walked down the ramp amid 100 other people and climbed on board for the 30-minute ride out to Schiphol. Luckily, we were able to find two seats together with room overhead for the luggage on an otherwise crowded train.

We got to the airport a couple of hours early, which gave us time to look at the shops and pick up a couple more things we didn't need, but somehow have to have when we're traveling. Mine was a piece of cheese covered with black pepper made in Holland.

Even though I had just been through this airport a few days earlier, I was again amazed at the size of the small city, the number of shops, and the endless mob of people who seemed to be going everywhere.

I was looking forward to getting on that plane and having an undisturbed nine hours in a seat. At last, we were on board and settled in for the long flight over the North Pole and down into Edmonton.

Joy watched a couple of movies to pass the time. I tried to watch something but was unable to concentrate. I just relaxed the best I could and tried to sleep.

Of course, I had no idea I was literally "walking death." I sincerely hope that I did not infect anyone else with my misery. It was likely ok because Joy, who sat next to me, escaped the disease.

It turned out that nine hours is a long time to be sitting on an airplane staring at the seatback in front of you. Nonetheless, time passes and after some fitful dozing, lots of staring at the flight tracker, and some intermittent conversation with Joy, we were getting ready to land at home.

Chapter 3

Day 2 – Edmonton, Alberta

Westbound polar flights are magic. You land at nearly the same time that you take off. We left at 3:30 pm on Tuesday, and at 4:30 pm, we arrived one-third of the way around the world.

I suppose if the plane was fast enough, you might land before you took off. In any case, after nine hours in the air, we were in Edmonton with the rest of the day in front of us.

We took our luggage, got a cab, and went home. We had put Cooper, our rambunctious nine-month-old Australian shepherd, in a nice boarding place for puppies during our two-week absence, so the house was quiet.

We decided to leave Cooper at the kennel for one more night so that we could have some peace. You don't realize how rambunctious and time-consuming a puppy is until they're absent for a while.

We really enjoyed the stillness. Our other dog greeted us wildly, and our two cats were also waiting to get their share of attention.

The only "serious illnesses" I'd ever experienced were measles and chickenpox as a kid. The flu, which I've only contracted two or three times, might've kept me in bed for three or four days at a stretch.

Gallbladder surgery, 18 months prior, with an already severely infected gallbladder, kept me in the hospital four days, and in bed for three more when I got home.

That was the sum of my experience with any "prolonged illness." The idea there might be some life-threatening monstrosity quietly waiting to kill me never even crossed my mind.

I guess we never think about that stuff, do we?

The flight had been restful, and I felt like I was on the mend. I went downstairs to the studio to check on my coaching schedule for the rest of the week. We had dinner and watched a little TV.

At the end of the evening, we were pleasantly reminiscing about all the places we'd been as we unpacked our haul of cool souvenirs. We were also talking about where we'd go next; we'd definitely do a cruise again.

As I got ready for bed, I started to feel a bad again, and a sense of foreboding crept into my heart.

Chapter 4

Day 3 – Edmonton

It was another rough night. The fever returned with a vengeance. I felt something was completely out of order, or it was a nasty flu.

Wednesday morning, I knew I was sick, and there was no way to pretend that this was getting better. I decided to stay in bed all day and treat it like the heavy-duty flu.

I knew I wasn't going to be able to keep any of my coaching calls that day, so, I pulled up my calendar and canceled all my calls but one.

I had one client I knew I just *had* to talk to. I decided to sleep until 4:30 pm when the call was scheduled, then get up and have the call come hell or high water.

Well, hell and high water came. My symptoms got worse, and I found myself feeling sicker than I have ever been before this.

I began to wonder how many days I would be laid up with this flu, how it would affect my schedule, and worried about notifying clients for the days to come.

Fortunately, I only coach on Monday, Tuesday, and Wednesday, so most of Thursday and Friday were already empty.

I had one other client that I had moved to Thursday who I just had to speak with. So, I decided again that no matter what, I would get up Thursday morning and have that call.

At 4:30 pm I got out of bed and washed up to prepare myself for the only remaining Wednesday call. I focused on the needs of that client, and the desire I had to serve them. I dragged myself downstairs and was blessed to be able to keep it together for an hour.

I learned two things from that experience. First, even if I was very sick, I was able, at least for a short period, to stay focused. I felt happy that I had served him.

The second thing was that I was, really, *really* sick. Still feverish, I slogged back upstairs and went to bed for the rest of the evening.

I was getting worried.

Chapter 5

Day 4 – Edmonton

During the night, I decided I'd better go to the doctor. The night was restful enough so that when I woke up the next morning, things didn't seem quite so bad – I felt better.

I still had a terrible cough and was coughing up ugly green mucus, but hey, it was just the flu, and I had no interest in sitting for an hour or two in the waiting room of a medical clinic.

I reasoned that I could lay in bed to better advantage and take care of myself and let my body heal. As you know, the body is incredible; it's astoundingly capable of healing. It was the wrong decision because there are times when you can't do it by yourself.

This morning, I was supposed to go to a meeting. It was part of a BNI business networking group to which I belong. I knew that was a bad idea.

First, I couldn't go because of how I felt. Second, I was sure none of them would want to have the slightest risk of getting whatever the heck it was I had.

I canceled everything for the day except for one single call, got dressed and went downstairs to my office for that one coaching call.

Unlike the day before, I was unable to hide the fact that I was sick, but the client was empathetic. It turned out to be a good thing I had the call because of his need, and he was also kind, given my condition.

For some reason, I kept thinking things would be ok. I put off going to the doctor another day, deciding that a good night's sleep, combined with the weekend would get the job done. That would give me Friday, Saturday and Sunday to rest, and allow me to recover.

Procrastination and pretending life will get better is a common reason we avoid doing things we know we should probably do. It is true in my coaching work, and I was doing that here with my health.

Chapter 6

Day 5 – Edmonton

By the time Friday morning rolled around I knew I had to go to the doctor. I was not getting better, and in fact, my symptoms were getting worse in ways I didn't understand.

I had a raging cough; the fever was severe, and the stuff I was coughing up was a horrifying color.

I got up at around 9:00 am, just before the doctor's office opened and got ready to go. I knew they would panic at the cough I had and because of how I looked. They have a sign in the clinic that reads "Anyone with a severe cough or flu-like symptoms, please notify the receptionist immediately."

I didn't want to scare anyone so when we got to the clinic, Joy went inside and asked for the nurse assistant to come outside to see me.

She got to the car, took one look at me and said "Don't even come in. Go straight to emergency. We'd have to send you there anyway, and it will save time."

Before she had arrived at the car, I had been coughing and had spit some phlegm on the ground next to the car. She saw that and ask if the spit was mine. I said "yes," and she replied, "please don't spit on the ground anymore, use a tissue."

Given the refusal to let me in, the urgency of her tone and my rapidly deteriorating physical condition I was starting to be genuinely concerned.

We got to the emergency room late in the morning; there was the usual group of people there for various reasons.

In every emergency room, it's common practice to have an initial conversation with an intake nurse to see how bad off you are. You're triaged so they can put you in a proper order based on the severity of your illness or injury.

Walk-ins are be prioritized with those arriving in ambulances, and everything is triaged according to need. My experience has been that this takes two or three hours.

Eighteen months earlier, I showed up in debilitating pain with a severely infected gallbladder, and it took two hours to get out of the ER waiting room and into a bed.

I expected nothing different now. Joy had dropped me off and told me to call her when I got admitted because she had to run a couple of errands to get ready for the weekend and wasn't feeling well herself.

To my surprise, it wasn't 10 minutes before they came and got me. They took me straight to a place I didn't even know existed in emergency rooms.

Every emergency room I had ever visited in my life, including this one, is a large room containing beds separated by curtains hanging from ceiling tracks. Everything is done, including undressing, examination, IV work and everything else – with the little privacy afforded by the curtains.

Instead, they had taken me to a separate and private room, which only added to my concern.

The nurse took my vitals and asked me questions about how long I had been ill, when it started, and what had occurred during the illness.

I told her we had finished a trip to Europe, including a cruise around the Baltic Sea. I listed the cities we visited and told her that the symptoms had started on Monday, 5 days earlier.

She took notes and said the doctor would be in shortly.

I lay there and waited for the doctor. I expected this to be another hour because that's what I had experienced every other visit to the ER, even when I had severely cut myself in a ski accident and needed stitches.

Once again, I was shocked when the doctor appeared in about 10 minutes.

Chapter 7

Day 5

University of Alberta Hospital

Edmonton, Alberta

A doctor took my vitals, looked over what had been done, and asked a few questions. I told him about the cruise, listed every city we visited, and everything that had happened, including the heat exhaustion a few days before. I also described as best I could the progression of the illness over the last few days.

After listening to my lungs, he looked grave, and I began to realize that this was a serious situation. He told me they were going to admit me to the hospital; there was no question about that. The only issue was where to find a room quickly.

The doctor returned in 10 minutes or so and said they thought I had pneumonia in both lungs and it looked terrible. He said I might need to be in intensive care for treatment. He repeated some of the earlier questions, focusing on the cities I had visited, and what I had done there that might have caused this illness.

I told him everything I could remember, which was nothing of any importance. He left, and I waited for a while lost in thought. I don't know how long it was, but it must have been a couple of hours.

A nurse and an orderly came to get me, said they had found a room and moved me up to the fifth floor, and then lifted me onto the bed.

A different doctor came in just a little while later and confirmed the diagnosis – severe pneumonia in both lungs. He stressed that it was very likely I'd end up in Intensive Care. I was lucky to have come in when I did.

Then he asked a question I had never been asked before. The implications were terrifying. "Do we have permission to do whatever we need to, including intubation, to treat you and preserve your life and health?"

I said yes, and he left. I was moved to consider what the implications of that question might be.

I updated Joy on the diagnosis and everything else. We went back and forth a bit, and neither one of us understood how dangerous the situation was. Not even close.

Once I was alone, I began to focus inward to see what I could sense. Breathing was staggeringly difficult, and I knew something was happening. As I focused on my body, I began to notice strange sensations.

I've practiced meditation for more than 45 years, and I'm extremely tuned into every nuance of feeling and physical sensation. I've used meditation to heal several illnesses over the years, including a proposed back surgery that I ultimately didn't need.

As I lay there and focused on my body, I could tell something was happening. I began to feel separation. It's difficult to describe, but it felt like the essence of my spirit and my soul, was separating from my body a piece at a time.

It was an unnerving and even frightening sensation which I'd never experienced before. It was slow, but the movement and feelings were apparent. At first, I didn't understand what was going on. After an hour or so, I realized I was in the process of dying.

I picked up my phone to send Joy a message. I'd lost all track of time, but I guess by now it was 11 pm or later. I sent her a brief text message with only three lines:

"ICU"

"Isolation – intubation."

"I may die."

Joy was at home and already in bed, so she didn't see the messages. She had been ill herself with mild cold symptoms, so she needed the sleep.

I don't remember much after that. I either went to sleep or lost consciousness. Sometime in the next hour or two, I was transported to the Intensive Care Unit (ICU) and put on life support.

Chapter 8

Day 6 through 8

University of Alberta Hospital ICU

The following chapters completing Section 1 are not from memory. I'm writing what Joy experienced as she described what happened after she left me in the emergency room and during the subsequent two weeks as I lay unconscious and on life support.

Friday, the day I went to the emergency room, at about 4:30 pm, I texted Joy and let her know what room I was being moved into. I told her that the doctor said I had severe pneumonia in both lungs and I'd be here for a few days. I told her about my labored breathing and that the doctor said they were considering moving me to the ICU.

At about 2:00 AM, Saturday morning, Joy got a phone call. It was the Hospital asking, "Are you coming?" The nurse told her I had been intubated, moved to the intensive care unit and that I had one of the worst cases of pneumonia she had ever seen. Hardly encouraging.

Joy heard the words but didn't understand what they meant. She told the nurse that she was sick and didn't think it was a good idea to come down. They agreed, but the nurse told her to come in the next day.

That's the last phone call in the world you want to get in the middle of the night. You have a loved one in the hospital; the hospital calls you and asks if you're coming.

She also saw my earlier cryptic text, and after talking with the nurse, sent me an answer, which I didn't see until a month later. "You're not going to die on my watch."

Joy got up the next morning and quickly went to the hospital to see what was happening.

Neither my ominous message, nor the nurse's explanation, nor Joy's imagination could have prepared her for what she saw. I had indeed been placed in intensive care. On top of that, I was in the Infectious Disease unit, like a "biohazard containment" facility you'd see in a movie.

Everyone is gowned, gloved and masked, and the rooms are under negative pressure so no air can escape. You had to go through two sets of double-door airlocks to get into the room.

The sight that greeted her was worse than she possibly could have imagined. I was laying on the bed, restrained, unconscious, with tubes down my throat and IVs protruding all over.

They didn't know what was causing my rapid decline in life force and vitality. They could tell that it was an aggressive and nasty infection that had attacked both my lungs and was now in my bloodstream.

They assembled an infectious disease team, and as Joy described it, "It was like a scene from a movie with people rushing around everywhere, trying this, trying that, seeing if anything could stabilize the vital signs and stop the decline."

They administered the most potent and versatile antibiotics available while continuing lab work to try to figure out what was going on.

Joy stayed at the hospital until about 2:00 pm. She went home for four hours to take care of our pets and do the things necessary to keep life moving on the outside.

She came back about 6:00 pm and stayed until she fell asleep on the couch at 1:00 am. The nurse gently woke her and asked if she didn't think it was time to go home and get some better sleep.

She repeated this routine Sunday and Monday. She monitored my blood pressure and vital signs like a hawk and asked the staff questions to try to understand what was happening and what the outcome might be.

What the doctors didn't tell her was that those first four days were touch-and-go, as I sat on the border between life and death.

They did tell her that there was no change and that I had stopped getting worse. At this point, any worse would mean death.

During those hours while she kept watch, she read me Scriptures, she read me my own writings, played music that I had on my phone, and talked to me. She assured me that I would not die. When my blood pressure got too high, she pestered the nurses until they did something about it.

She got to know everyone on the staff personally and was unflagging in her love and devotion.

I weep as I write this when I think tenderly upon this scene, this precious woman praying, talking, encouraging, pestering and doing everything that could be humanly done and divinely possible to save my life.

What she couldn't have known then was that during those days when I was so close to death, I was indeed at the boundary between this life and eternity.

On three different days, I had conversations with God at the doorway between life and death. I'll describe those conversations, their content, and meaning in detail in Part Two.

For now, on the outside, the drama unfolded.

Chapter 9

Day 8 through 9

University of Alberta Hospital ICU

Monday evening the infectious disease team told her that they had isolated and identified the pathogen. I had contracted a case of community-acquired necrotizing MRSA, (Methicillin-resistant Staphylococcus aureus) a horribly aggressive, antibiotic-resistant, usually lethal strain of staph bacteria.

Fortunately, the antibiotics they had been administering while they did the testing were the right ones, so they simply continued what they were already doing. MRSA kills more people than AIDS, and it is a growing lethal threat.

Discovering the cause and knowing that the treatment was on the right track was a huge relief. The worrisome part was that nothing changed. I hovered between life and death for some time.

While the doctors kept reporting, "no change," Joy chose to view it as a favorable prognosis. At least it wasn't getting worse. The head of the infectious disease team finally told her that he didn't expect to see any improvement for several days, at the earliest, which provided Joy with additional relief.

At this point, no one knew whether I would live or die. It was unclear how long I'd be on life support, how long I'd be unconscious, or how long it would take to start improving.

Joy also requested that the elders from our church come and give me a blessing, which they did. I am quite sure that this request also had something to do with the conversations I'll describe in later chapters.

Chapter 10

Days 9 -19 – ICU

At one point, frustrated that the bacteria count was not decreasing, the medical personnel started looking for additional problems. They discovered that the MRSA bacteria was growing inside one of the tubes in my neck. That is an incredible hallmark of how aggressive this bacterium can be.

The next step was to remove the tubes from one side of my head and put them on the other side. The incredible diligence of this team and my precious companion were indispensable. Apparently, the MRSA bacteria loves to attach itself to plastic tubing.

As previously mentioned, left untreated, the 10-day mortality rate for this infection is 100%. That means without treatment by Wednesday; I would have been dead.

Even with hospitalization, the 10-day mortality rate is still 60%. We had come in on day five. Not a good prognosis. Nevertheless, (as you've already guessed) I didn't die, and I now have the opportunity to tell the story and write this book.

During the next ten days, Joy's routine never varied. She got up in the morning, took care of our pets, the necessary tasks in the house and came to the hospital.

Her vigil usually started by 9:00. By now, the medical team all knew her well. During these ten days, she also saw three people die in other rooms in the ICU.

Because of a problem with the power system in one of the rooms, the staff moved me to a room where someone had just passed away. Joy was not sure how she felt about being put in a room where someone had just died, but ultimately that's where we ended up.

Getting into the isolation rooms is a significant process. You can't just walk in. You have to call and report who you are, why you're there, and get permission from the medical staff to enter.

You then go through a set of airlock doors into the interior area. You then have to suit up and go through another set of double doors to get actually into the room with the patient.

The sterile gloves gave Joy a severe rash. The masks were stifling but had to be worn at all times. Regardless of these discomforts, she showed up day after day to hold my hand, tell me stories, read me sacred literature and be there with her presence.

Finally, my condition began to improve.

It eventually became clear that I probably wasn't going to die. Then it became clear that I would not die. Now it was just a process of continuing the antibiotics and waiting for the body and the medicine to do the magic.

In this area in the hospital, each patient has a dedicated nurse, who is with you for 12 hours at a time. Every 12 hours, a different ICU nurse comes on shift and the cycle repeats. The dedication of these people to care for others is astounding. The nurse does nothing but look after your welfare, your vitals and the things that are needed to keep you alive and on the mend.

As the days progressed, Joy says they periodically woke me from an induced coma. She says they asked my name, asked me to squeeze fingers and wiggle toes to evaluate progress.

I don't remember any of these events, but I do remember the awful and terrifying hallucinations.

I'm hard of hearing and usually wear powerful hearing aids. Somehow, during this coma, my hearing seemed amplified; I could hear sounds and voices everywhere.

I could hear conversations and was convinced that conspiracies were afoot and that I was in far more trouble than just being in the hospital at death's door. Somehow, my life had become the focus of intense investigation, and every that every skeleton imagined was dragged from the closet and amplified.

I understand now that these hallucinations are common, but at the time there was nothing I could do, and the terror was heart stopping. Even though I was restrained for my own safety, some of the hallucinations were of me up walking around.

One particularly vivid hallucination was during the Christmas season, choosing ornaments and decorating trees. In the hallucination, I was naked and somehow couldn't find any clothes.

The nurse assigned to me for that day was somehow part of the hallucination, and for some reason had left me alone. It was snowing in the room, I was getting cold, and I was sure that wandering around in the snow I would soon freeze to death.

We do live in Edmonton, where winters are long and sometimes the temperature drops to -40°C. I guess it's worthy of the term, "The Frozen North," but this was the middle of June.

The number and type of these hallucinations would fill a volume by itself. They were not pleasant, physically visceral, and always scary. I mention them here only because they were so vivid and terrifying.

Some might say that the conversations with God in the next chapter were merely additional hallucinations. I address this here because nothing could be further from the truth. The hallucinations I am describing were agonizing, physically painful and always scary.

If I gave them a color, they would be black. They were hazy, confusing and at the opposite end of the spectrum from the setting and the feelings that accompanied the conversations with God at the door.

Other than the very brief periods of consciousness described above, to keep me connected with reality, the first two weeks in the hospital were spent on life support under sedation. Eventually, my condition improved sufficiently to take me off the tubes and return me to consciousness.

Joy was encouraged. We were coming to the end of the time where I was completely sedated and physically restrained, so as not to accidentally yank tubing out and do other things that would cause harm to myself.

When the bronchial tubes and the rest of the apparatus was removed, they decided it was necessary to cut a hole in my throat and put in a tracheal tube, in case something took a sudden turn for the worse.

When it came time to do this procedure, the doctor asked Joy if she wanted to watch. He told her she could stay if she didn't mind the blood. She politely excused herself and decided to get lunch.

She had no interest in watching them cut a hole in my throat and put new tubing, albeit less than before, in my body.

On the outside, a medical miracle had occurred. The doctors and nurses had performed with nonstop diligence and had saved me from certain death.

My precious wife had spent every waking hour attending me and encouraging me to live. Members of my faith had visited, administered blessings and done everything they could to encourage Joy in her vigil.

All this outpouring of service and love is a hallmark both of the professionalism of the medical staff and of the kindness of all of those people who know us.

As this drama was playing out in the physical world, I was in a multi-day dance with the Grim Reaper and ultimately gained freedom from his grasp.

The other sacred story that was playing out was inside, where my spirit had several conversations with the Almighty. Choices were laid out, commitments made, and now it was time for me to rejoin the conscious world and merge the two separate stories into one.

Part II – The Door to Eternity

We've all heard stories about near-death experiences. We sometimes wonder if they're real. We wonder why they happen to some, and not others.

From what I had heard and read, combined with my own experiences, I knew that such things were not only possible but likely. I also thought that many, if not most of the reported cases were true.

All the near-death experiences I was acquainted with had a purpose, a message, a call to opportunity. They offer a revelation or guidance that must come from the spiritual to the physical realm. Each experience created a purpose or change for the better.

Even with all this, and with substantial revelations and spiritual experiences of my own, I never expected to have such an overpowering experience.

Now that it has happened, I am grateful beyond words, and at the same time, seriously committed to discovering every piece of information and value and sharing that with the world.

To do something less would dishonor the sacred nature of the experience, and the power of what I heard and the actions I committed to complete.

Given that God is almighty and can do whatever occurs to Him, how these things take place is beyond my understanding. I'm content to have it remain so until I do pass into that eternal realm.

There I hope to gain further understanding about the order of things on this side of the veil as well as the other side, and elsewhere in the universe.

Until then, I can only report what happened, what I felt, what I heard, what I learned, what I committed to doing and what I know for myself to be true and real.

Chapter 11

Awakening – Location Unknown

I was laying on the floor, or, at least I *think* it was the floor. I was not aware of what was under me, but I was horizontal when awareness crystallized. The place seemed infinitely large. I couldn't see walls or other structures in any direction.

Everything felt gentle and soft. Not spongy soft like a cushion or a couch, but emotionally soft and calm. There were no sounds. There was only consciousness. There was consuming quiet and peace.

All other times during my coma there was always anxiety. I saw, felt and heard things that were cold, frightening and unclear even though I could never tell exactly what they were.

I'm hard of hearing, but in these troubled states, my hearing seemed sharpened; whispers and voices seemed to be everywhere. The overwhelming color to describe the feelings of all these other semi-conscious states is inky, visceral, smothering black.

In stark contrast, at *this* moment of consciousness, everything was utterly peaceful and still. There was a sense of safety and power.

In my field of vision—a bit distant and slightly to the left—a doorway seemed to materialize. I couldn't see walls or anything connected to the doorway. It was merely a doorway. On the other side was intense white light.

Unlike sunlight, it didn't stream through the doorway to illuminate my side of the opening. Looking through the doorway, I could see white light. It was not blinding in nature, it was just white, and it felt clean and inviting.

I felt a yearning to go to the doorway but wasn't sure how to get there. There was no floor or at least none that I could see, and I wasn't sure I could stand up.

As I thought this, I found myself instantly in the doorway, standing upright and looking into the light. I was leaning ever so slightly against the doorjamb, and I was completely relaxed as I focused my eyes on the opening.

I didn't feel any compulsion to step through the doorway, or any fear. I was content to be there, waiting and gazing into the light.

I then became aware of a person on the other side. The person was standing so close to me that I could've reached out and touched them, but I didn't move my arms. I couldn't make out facial features, but I was unquestionably in the presence of God.

I was at peace, suspended in time and space, separated by less than an arm's length from such holiness and power that I cannot articulate the feeling. Words utterly fail me as I try to describe the circumstance. Emotion wells up as I write this and re-experience the peace, power, and presence that I felt.

Chapter 12

The First Conversation at the Door

I don't know how long I stood there, staring into the light, looking at the visage on the other side. I still felt no yearning to step through, nor did I feel a compulsion to reach out and touch the person. I was merely content to stand there and be in the presence of such peace. After a time, I both heard and felt a question.

"Do you want to come home?"

There was no explanation or further elaboration, but I knew, without the slightest doubt, that it was an invitation to step across the threshold into eternity. The question was as straightforward as it was unexpected. It just hung in the air without explanation and expectation.

I was utterly taken aback, and for a long time had no idea where to even begin deliberation in my mind, let alone explain what I was thinking to Him who had posed it. There was no sense of urgency. There was no expectation about a response. It was just a question that I knew needed an answer.

At various points in my life, the idea of meeting God created different feelings, depending on the situation I was in at the time. When I was addicted to cocaine and living an entirely hedonistic life, the thought of meeting God never crossed my mind.

If I had thought about it, I suppose it would have struck me with abject terror. My best defense during that period of life was not to think about it and do whatever I was doing with reckless abandon and the illusion that it would never end.

At other times, when I felt like I was trying to do what I thought I "should" do and be whom I thought I "should" be, I did occasionally think about meeting God. Generally, it was a fearful thought, because I never felt like I was "good enough."

In those times, my mind was clouded and harrowed up by thoughts of recent misdeeds, places and times where I had failed to live up to some standard.

In more recent years, the thought of meeting God was peaceful and not accompanied by fear or worry. I was confident that I was doing what I could to fill the measure of my creation. Whatever the reason, I felt no anxiety or fear in any way at either the encounter nor the question hanging in the air.

I began to consider what such a choice would entail.

My first thoughts were of my wife, Joy. If I said "yes" and passed into eternity, she would be left alone. I knew she would be heartbroken. I also knew that if I passed into eternity, God would not abandon her. There would be a way that she, working with God, would get through this hardship and go on to live a happy and productive life.

As I considered everything, I just wasn't ready to leave her even though I was sure whatever would come would be wonderful. The most potent yearning that I felt respecting Joy was about the things we were doing and had planned to do together in the service of God.

For nearly a year, we've been facilitators of a 12-Step addiction recovery program sponsored by our church. It has been an excellent source of satisfaction and fulfillment. I'd finally found a way to give back to others some of the help I had received during my addictions.

We had plans to serve other missions for the church and to spend the rest of our lives in the service of God. My soul yearned to have the experiences that we had discussed and planned for and so frequently and so excitedly. I really didn't want to miss that part of my mortal life.

I thought about our finances, and how ill-prepared we were to have either one of us pass through the veil and leave the other alone. Note to self: get better financially organized! The stark reality of the effects of procrastination paraded through my mind.

As all these thoughts passed through my mind, I realized just how deeply and passionately and fervently I love this woman. I realized how much I would miss her, and how much I treasure the sound of her voice and the warmth of her body as we sleep together. I cherish the conversations we have as we drive, particularly on long trips.

We had driven 1,800 miles one-way from Phoenix to Edmonton and back more times than I could count. Each of these trips had been rich with conversation and experience as we got to know each other better and shared thoughts about our future together.

I was not prepared to have all that precious experience with this woman end. We are married in the Temple for all eternity, and I know that I will have her as my wife in the eternal world. Even with that knowledge, I wanted more, now, in this mortal frame.

We are running three or four successful businesses and having fun as partners. We get to work together every day from home. I couldn't imagine suddenly being without all this and not continuing the work we were doing together. There was just so much more to do.

Next, I thought about my kids. My long and tumultuous past with multiple failed relationships has left many of my children estranged. This estrangement has been a continuous source of sadness and motivation for me. Different kids blame me in varying degrees for every problem in their lives. My longing is to love and support them, and there is still much that needs doing.

It is sadly true that I made many spectacular mistakes. I was not the kind of parent that I had always imagined I would be. Despite my childhood experience, I had sworn that no matter what, I would not be the cause of pain or misery in my children's lives.

Because of the violence of my upbringing, I had been through 45 years of depression, most of it undiagnosed and untreated. My parental fantasy skills had never materialized. There are countless things that I would do differently if I could re-do parts of my life.

After decades of mental illness, I had finally determined that I needed help and had done the necessary things to get clean and treat the depression and its consequences. However, the relationships are still a work in progress. I've finally come to realize that every person makes choices about what they will and won't do to create and maintain connections. I can't force that to happen in any way.

I recognize that they are adults and are making choices for their own lives about what they do and do not want to spend their time doing. So, while it's entirely not true that I am responsible for the poor choices they make now, I felt a longing to have more time to create future opportunities and potential reconciliation.

I wanted more time to be open and available so that they might make different choices and allow us the opportunity to share joyful family companionship once again.

There are ten amazing kids. Yes, ten of them. Each, with their spouses or "significant others" and some with their own kids. One at a time, they went through my mind, and I lovingly saw faces and heard voices. I must have more opportunities.

I thought about the clients whom I am currently serving. Again, faces and voices passed before my face, and I felt incomplete. I didn't think that I had given less than 100%, but I had a great desire to do more for them, and for many clients yet unserved.

I meditate regularly, and when I do, I sense the presence of many others yet to be served. Again, the feeling of incompleteness came over me and made me feel all the more that I wanted to stay.

I'm in the middle of writing four books, not counting this one. Also, not counting the other book that eventually came from these experiences called, *The Book of Context.*

I have 33 songs that are mostly written and are in various stages of recording. These songs are a companion to the trilogy that started with *Tightrope.* It's certainly not that I think my creative output will change the world, but I know I was directed to do this work and it's not yet finished.

I thought about my own family of origin: my mother and my siblings. There has been significant animosity toward me because I wrote the *Tightrope of Depression* which is about my struggle with mental illness and exposed the violence that took place in my formative years.

I was not prepared to leave the world with that situation as it is. I wanted more time. Not to change what I had written, but to work more to have love overtake misunderstanding.

All these things considered, there was a sense of incompleteness and mostly of huge opportunity. There was so much left to do, and so much I wanted to create. I felt that I wasn't ready to go.

It wasn't an unsettling feeling or one of distress; it was merely a peaceful certainty that I still had work to do. Some I had already committed to God to accomplish and some I had chosen to undertake for myself. I also had the absolute certainty that there was much more I didn't even know about yet.

After considering all these things carefully, I explained that I felt incomplete and wanted to stay here on Earth. I knew that there was peace and comfort and tranquility on the other side, but I felt like my time had not come.

I chose to stay.

After I made my explanation, I felt contentment, like I had thoroughly considered what was left to do to fill the work He had for me. I also felt leaving now would be somewhat selfish.

I am a disciple of Jesus Christ. I am committed to following him at all hazards. Given that commitment, I felt like if I bailed on my unfinished business, then I hadn't really given my whole soul.

Sometimes I the conversation was verbal, and at other times it only appeared in my thoughts. Sometimes it was difficult to tell. I suppose communication on the other side of the veil might be everything wrapped into one.

I don't remember exactly how the first conversation ended, but all was quiet and peaceful, as it should be. I felt I had done "the right thing," if with our limited understanding we are even capable of determining what that might be.

Reflecting on this extraordinary experience, I found it both interesting and joyful that there was never any consideration of whether I was "prepared," or "good enough" to move on. That worry was often the main theme earlier in life, and it had terrified me to think about standing before Christ or God for evaluation or "judgment."

It's a joyful thing that the conversations were all about things that were present, and things I wanted to create for the future. I didn't feel guilty or convicted for past mistakes.

This isn't to imply that there is no responsibility for our choices. I am sure that there is a real element of accountability for how we use our "right to choose," but it demonstrated God's willingness to forgive, and the power of our effort to improve our lives.

It occurred to me afterward that the old song of guilt was never part of the conversation. It was about whether I "wanted" to stay. The choice was mine.

Chapter 13

The Second Conversation at the Door

Part 1

The next day, I found myself again at the door. I was speaking with the same person in the same doorway. I don't know how I knew a day had passed, and I have no proof; I just accepted it as truth.

I was there at the door and prepared to receive further learning, love, and direction.

The question of the previous day seemed to be a settled issue as we started. This conversation was by far the longest of the three and consisted of two distinct parts. I will describe them in separate chapters.

The feelings and context around the conversation were of gentleness, love, and kindness. We don't have the words to describe the depth and power of the emotions, but they were consuming and communicated ultimate peace.

There was an earnestness about the situation coming from God that made me aware of his sincere desire for my happiness and success.

There were three things that I somehow knew as absolutes in this conversation. They were communicated to me in ways I cannot describe. Partly spoken, partly felt and completely understood. There is a communication that happens in the soul so powerful that words pale, doubts evaporate, and you just *know* certain things.

The first thing I learned, felt and heard is the most critical, fundamental condition of life. It is that God loves us beyond our ability to comprehend.

That meant he loves *me*.

As a condition of my depression, I often considered myself unworthy or undeserving of His love. I also frequently believed that I had, through my own actions, created an unbreachable barrier between myself and the divine.

My first learning was that this assumption was not right. As I said before, none of my past mistakes, willful disobedience or rebellion was in any way part of the fabric of any of the conversations.

The second fundamental learning was a clear understanding that it is God's earnest desire and purpose to provide us with the opportunity for growth, development, and happiness.

There is order in the universe, and this development is not random. It doesn't take place according to rules of our own making but follows the pattern that exists independently in this universe.

I was reminded of a science-fiction movie where a traveler was suddenly in contact with massively more evolved and perfected intelligent beings who were showing the universe to this newcomer in fantastic and grand ways.

The traveler, overwhelmed with the beauty and power asked, "Can't you show this to everyone?"

The higher intelligence responded, "This is the way it is to be done."

There's nothing comparable in any of our imaginations, books or movies to the experience of being in the presence of the Almighty. This little analogy seems a demonstration of our inability to comprehend that the universe and God are the way they are, and our desire to re-create them according to our wishes is merely a waste of time. It's a distraction, and ultimately a barrier to our understanding and development.

The third moving and powerful message was: all the things that had happened in my life had happened for a reason.

- The abusive upbringing in the name of religion had shaped to me in ways that I could now use in service to others.

- The depression and self-loathing of my childhood had plagued me for decades. Now it would be a springboard of compassion that would let me develop more patience and kindness in service.

- My failed relationships, and all the poor choices and sadness surrounding them, had given me empathy that would increase my ability to understand and serve.

- My addictions to drugs and alcohol helped me prepare and understand those who would suffer similar or related problems.

- Even this illness had brought me to the place where I stood face to face with God to be taught about the truth of my existence, my purpose, and ultimately the path to pure joy and fulfillment.

That is not to say that God designed and put me through all those difficulties. The choices of others and my selfish weakness, combined with the vagaries of the world, bring us all into difficult, terrifying and sometimes life-threatening circumstances.

The point is: rather than be angry, curse God, and blame others, I was instructed to use *all* these things, and allow them to shape my soul, my heart, and increase the love and empathy I have.

I was instructed to blame no one, cease to carry any resentment, anger or frustration about anything that had happened or would happen in the future.

The beauty of all this is the absolute certainty that God, with his infinite power and wisdom, can take any occurrence in our lives and shape it to our benefit.

From this moment on, my life was changed. This focus and purpose were given at this time as an extension of the things that had been happening over the last several years, in preparation for this moment.

In February of this year, in meditation, I was impressed to create a "Personal Truth and Commitment" (PTAC). This is a *declaration* of whom I choose to be in the world, and a *commitment* to live according to that declaration, at all hazards.

I had worked on it for several months and created a powerful and meaningful document. I read it frequently to keep focused and progress on what I feel called to do in the world. The creation of this guide was one example which illustrated the direction the preparation had been taking.

The content of such a statement is highly personal, and ultimately a declaration that you make about yourself, not for anyone else. It needs no one's approval but your own since it is *your* choice and *your* commitment.

I do not include my PTAC statement here. It's highly personal and is also beyond the scope of this book. If you want to know more about the creation of a PTAC, I have included a page at the end of the book with contact information, and we can have a conversation.

Another clear piece of preparation was: I had been driven over the last several years to be in the coaching business. In my previous executive career, I occupied many leadership positions but hadn't thought about the mentoring or coaching aspects of those responsibilities.

Some of those leadership qualities happened naturally, and some came as a result of training for the positions I held. I began to enjoy facilitating the success and development of others.

Because of my long history with music, I had often been asked to create and lead choirs in my church and community. I've taken great joy in helping a group of volunteers to learn to sing, sing parts, sing beautifully, and focus together as a unit.

In 20/20 hindsight I can now see the grand tapestry of preparation that moved me toward the coaching business and pushed me—despite my fears and selfish inclinations—in the direction of preparing for service.

All these things, combined with the sometimes barely audible but insistent invitations I've felt to be "more than I was," had brought me to the place that made this moment sweet beyond my ability to articulate.

Over the last three years, I have been writing books about my history. The first book, *TightRope of Depression*, details the first 55 years of my life, my long wrestle with Major Depressive Disorder (MDD) and the blessings and terrors of that affliction.

I've written eleven original songs for an album as a companion to *Tightrope*. After finishing the first book, I realized that a single volume was now complete. There will be a trilogy to complete the story, and I will be creating an album to accompany each of the three books. The second volume is, *Down from the Gallows*, and is about half done as of this writing.

I have had the distinct and repeated inspiration over the last two years that finishing these projects is of utmost importance, not only for my own development but also for my mission in the world.

Resentment and pushback from my family of origin and some of my kids have caused me to doubt the value of these projects. In this series of conversations, I was clearly and explicitly told that finishing these projects as quickly and thoroughly as possible, *right now*, is of the *utmost* importance.

This renews my dedication and commitment to spend my time in this pursuit.

Foundation principles I am instructed to emphasize are:

1. Forgiveness, for myself and others.

2. The rebuilding of damaged relationships.

3. Reaching out to offer love.

4. Reconciliation, rehabilitation and every other word that means inclusiveness, love, and the circle of completion in God's grand plan for his children.

I was instructed that the focus of my work is to live in service and to loudly and clearly proclaim the message that each person is a child of God. We are offspring of the Almighty.

Each of us has a mission that we got before we came here. We were given gifts and talents to do that assignment. We have a choice about walking that path, but this is why so many people feel called to "do something more" in their lives.

Is also means, because we are the offspring of God, we each have infinite potential and can be and do and create whatever we choose. The essential companion learning is that we are here to serve each other.

It occurred to me that my instructions are a precise mirror of how God treats us. Every action, instruction, and focus are given in love, for our development, advancement and ultimate joy. This is true even if some of the things seem complicated or difficult.

I don't have the words to describe the nuances, intensity, and depth of the instruction and power that was conveyed during this part of the conversation. I felt cradled in the arms of safety, and yet connected at all points in my spirit to the Infinite. This provided an influx of power and information that felt like a thousand fire hoses.

At the same time, there was absolute peace and purpose, and no sense of overwhelm. It was as if my spirit was connected to the pure divinity of the universe and could accept and comprehend all these things at the same instant in time.

This experience was one of kindness and joy. I knew what I needed to do for my own preparation. I knew the things I must leave behind.

Previously, I measured success by cash, cars, powerful positions, and many of the traditional material yardsticks. I was explicitly instructed that these are irrelevant and to stop measuring life in this fashion. Given this truth, I suddenly knew to my core that all the typical material measures of success no longer mattered.

In the first conversation, I decided to stay. The reasons that had been paramount in that deliberation were a concern for love for others, the creation or repair of relationships, and the establishment of good works in the world as far as I could make things happen.

God was full of love and concerned with the development, growth, and happiness of all his creations. Isn't that evident in the beauty of the world, the majesty of the mountains, the glory of growing things and the wonders manifest in the magic of the seasonal changes?

God is merciful and kind and without harsh judgment. How could I be any less?

How could I be less than patient and understanding with myself and with others as I seek personal development and to be a catalyst for love and growth in those I'm blessed to interact with?

I knew that my decision to remain was the right one and I grew more and more focused and excited about the things I needed to do. At the same time, I was committing to do, to be more of what God had created me to be.

Even though I was confident that I was doing the right things and that all these developmental processes were ones I wanted, and eagerly committed to, I also knew it would be work.

As I contemplated the magnitude of the changes involved, and how much there was to do, I felt the assurance that this was a partnership. As long as I sought, listened, and dared to act, God would be with me to complete these assignments.

Another undeniable truth washed over my soul. If all these glorious opportunities are true for me, they are true for *every single one* of God's other children. I was just given a chance to be a catalyst for some of those precious souls.

However, I also knew that the implementation and execution of these commitments were going to be an entirely different matter. I've spent 62 years on Earth, and know how often I've gotten sidetracked, distracted and forgotten things that I knew so certainly just a day before.

It wouldn't be until I got out of the hospital that I realized how literal some of the work would be in creating this development and following this path.

Chapter 14

The Second Conversation at the Door

Part 2

I felt encouraged, inspired and determined. I had big visions and could see opportunities and paths in all directions. The excitement vibrated all the way through my soul.

My coaching practice, the volunteer work with the church, the 12-Step program and other things that Joy and I were involved in are all perfect vehicles to make these things happen. At the same time, I was determined to have a greater focus, exert greater effort, create a larger circle of opportunity and be less sidetracked for trivialities.

I knew the work I am doing now is just the beginning, and that more opportunities to be of service would manifest as fast as I could make myself able to do them. It's funny, at another time I would've felt overwhelmed. Now, I was simply vibrating with excitement that I knew was not my own but was on loan from God.

The vision was reassuring, challenging, and exciting all at the same time. Somehow, I knew there was a way to do everything in wisdom, and in its own due time.

In contemplating all the things that I yearned to do to become the person God intended, the conversation turned to the following question.

As I do this work, and since I am both choosing and allowed to remain in the world, what can I do to both express gratitude and be of service to each beautiful soul that has been placed on the earth for their own development and joy?

We all know innately that we operate at merely a fraction of our potential. Sometimes that causes us to be frustrated or discouraged, and sometimes it's a cause for excitement and optimism.

Whichever we choose, when we sit quietly, we know that as divine beings we have limitless potential for creativity and adding good to the world.

I asked, "Why do we settle? Why do we simply allow ourselves to be satisfied with so little when you offer the secrets of the universe for the asking?"

This answer to this question began a revelation that will turn into another book. That book is "The Book of Context." It will explain the process I use to help others understand what's really possible for them.

It's one thing to say things like, "You can have whatever you want." Or, "you can be whatever you want to be," or, "You can create whatever life you can dream." It's quite another to provide the information, tools, and encouragement to allow that truth to emerge.

Limitless potential, which gets talked about so much these days, is either a myth or the truth. Which is it?

As I stood in the presence of God and gazed into the eternities of opportunity, I knew without question, that you and I and every other person comes to the earth with infinite possibilities and divine destiny.

As I considered this truth, I thought about all the different societies, economic conditions, cultures, and governments in the world today. Some are full of openness and opportunity. Others are full of oppression and despair.

That means that for some, the Earth journey is short, painful, even cruel. We don't have to look back very far in history to see hundreds of examples where the brutality of man limits our development.

On my own, I cannot change the injustice, cruelty, disappointment, and sadness of either the past or the present. This was driven home profoundly during our visit to Eastern Europe during the cruise.

We spent a day in Tallinn, Estonia. It's a beautiful, historic walled city. There were narrow cobblestone streets and buildings crammed together in the traditional style.

There were beautiful shops and merchants of all kinds selling things to tourists. Some locals went to different stores and went about their daily business. Tourists and tour groups were everywhere. On one street I saw a building with an open door with the sign on the doorpost above. As I got closer, I could read the sign, "Former KGB Black Site."

As I got to the door and looked in, there was a steep, narrow staircase that led down into the ground under the building at least 14 or 15 feet. I went down three or four steps to the reception desk and looked at the stark pictures on the wall. The museum was beyond the desk, and I could see a little way down the hallways that went right and left.

Waves of revulsion and horror washed over me as the emotional screams from the past blasted through my soul. I had no desire to see more and quickly left. Even without seeing, the thought of things that had happened there, and at hundreds of similar sites through thousands of years horrified me.

Such feelings can easily prevent me from feeling adequate or capable. What difference can I make in the world with such forces at play?

In my vision, the answer came with resounding clarity. It is a simple matter to commit to doing everything I can, with the people I meet and the opportunities I have.

I committed in the presence of God to take myself and my ego out of the equation and to do precisely what I felt at that moment.

Even knowing that I am only one person, I know that with a divine assignment and help, I *can* make a difference. History is full of individuals who did things that made a difference to many.

Even knowing that, as a human being I would stumble and fall over and over again. I found and cherished the excitement and courage to make such a commitment with full purpose of heart.

The alternative is not to try – or to give a halfhearted effort, or only choose easy situations to minimize the effort required or the possibility of failure.

Given my history of depression, addiction and other failures, and the patience and love that God had exhibited toward me in my journey of learning, how could I be satisfied with that choice?

My bad choices had been a source of cruelty, dishonesty, broken dreams, drug addiction, failure as a parent, and a host of other ills, yet somehow God in his mercy had forgiven me.

I also know from my own experience, that God can heal those we have injured, even when we cannot. He has the power to heal those pains and help them through the paths that they have to walk, if they want it, and if they are willing to forgive and seek their peace and healing.

I remembered a time in deep meditation and prayer that happened three years after I had begun my recovery from depression and determined to make my life more valuable.

Contemplating how much pain I had caused one particular person, and in my anguish, I asked God, "How can I possibly do anything to repair the damage I've caused to that person?"

The thought came swiftly and clearly. "You can't do anything to repair that person's heart, confidence, and trust, but I can." An overwhelming peace and certainty flooded my soul. At that moment I came to realize that regardless of our minimal ability to repair most of the things we've inflicted on others through our lifetimes, God can heal.

That thought, combined with my commitment to be and do everything that I could do from this moment on gave me the optimism, excitement, and courage I needed.

Now back to the question. "Why do we settle, when so much more is available?"

Again, the answer came swiftly and precisely. It is simple, yet rigorous. *We do not believe!*

As I study all the sacred literature from many traditions, the choice to *believe* is a foundational piece of both the power and the truth contained in that spiritual system.

Many say: "I don't believe that," or "I can't believe such a thing," or "I can't see it or prove it, so I can't believe it." Ultimately, that's a cop-out. I've had those thoughts myself many times. The truth is, here was God telling me that the foundational missing piece is a *choice* to believe.

We don't achieve the things that are possible because we don't believe we can.

So, what is it that we don't believe? In my case, and for many I work with, we don't think we're good enough. We don't believe we are skilled enough, or powerful enough, or competent enough, or whatever word you want to insert.

We do not accomplish that which we cannot believe. If something is entirely outside our beliefs, or our ability to believe, we don't even try. We don't formulate plans, look for opportunities, or look for the strength and energy needed to make something happen.

If we believe something is completely beyond our reach, then, of course, it turns out to be.

We have hundreds of sayings in our modern lexicon that emphasize this. For example:

1. "If you think you can or you think you can't, you're right."

2. "Whatever you believe you can achieve."

3. "As a man thinketh, so is he."

The difficulty comes when we relegate belief to mystical, supernatural or religious realms. Beliefs dominate every aspect of your life. You have beliefs woven into the fabric of your soul about money, meaning, worth, relationships, health, and every other part of your life.

Where the beliefs came from came from: be it family, socialization, religion, school, and everything else, is not the subject of this book, nor was it the subject of my conversation with God.

We live our lives glued to these beliefs, riveted to them, nailed to them, as if they were complete and absolute truth.

Every psychologist and medical professional will tell you that the biggest determining factor in the recovery from illness is whether the patient *believes* they can, and *desires* to recover.

One of the fundamental difficulties is this: we don't even believe that beliefs are the root of the problem. We are looking for anything else to be the solution to the freedom, prosperity, and joy we want.

Easy examples flashed through my mind during the conversation:

1. We believe we don't have time to do the things we "want" to do.

2. We believe we don't have the energy or power to make things happen that we dream.

3. We believe we don't have the skill or talent as others do.

4. We believe God loves others, but not us.

5. We believe we've made too many mistakes and our time has passed.

6. We believe that all the good luck is for someone else.

7. We believe things are too hard, so we don't try.

8. We start and fail and then pretend that's a signal that this task, accomplishment or dream just wasn't meant for us.

9. We believe it is not our lot to be, do, or have certain things.

10. We believe a thousand variations of these statements.

The mind and the body being completely obedient and accept these myths in such a way as to make them real. Thus, we are perfect examples of the truth that what we believe creates our reality.

We demonstrate this truth every day whether we mean to or not. It's just that we're using it in a negative way when we fail to create, rather than in a positive way to follow through with the act of creating.

The first and most profound problem is that we are generally unaware of the things we believe. They are woven so deeply into the fabric of our hearts and minds and habits that they're accepted as concrete barriers bounding what's possible.

So then, what do we do about all this? If all of those beliefs and their thousand variations are disempowering, and prevent us from being who we really can be, what do we believe instead?

The answer is simple.

Choose to believe that you are a divinely created being with a powerful and intentional purpose to your creation. That is the start. Believe that at the core of your soul. Do whatever you need to do to make that the centerpiece of your being.

Choose to believe that you have access to powers in the universe that are beyond your comprehension, but available for your use to add good to the world.

Choose to believe that you, individually, are valuable, worthy of love, and capable of creating amazing things you haven't even thought of yet.

Choose to believe that no matter what has happened to you, no matter where you've been, no matter how old you are or how young you are, that your opportunity has not passed, and the best part of your life is in front of you.

Some claim that "My experience has taught me otherwise." Whatever we have experienced is a fraction of what is available to experience, learn and know in the future. The future is *not* an extension of the past.

However often you have to repeat and revisit these beliefs to replace the old ones you might have, do it. The alternative is to accept the litany of things you believe today, which got you exactly where you are.

Desiring to believe and choosing to believe are only the first steps. Action, persistence, and courage are required to complete the equation.

Absolutely nothing can begin, and the fire can't be lit until you take the first step and choose to believe the fundamental truth that is before us all.

In this conversation, God made unequivocally clear that whatever each of us deeply believes can come to pass. Choosing to keep a belief in the impossibility of dreams and visions permanently perpetuates the present.

It is for this reason, and this reason alone, that we settle for far less than is available.

Lack of belief causes apathy; it causes laziness, it causes fear, which is the psychological state one step above death. It is the central and primary cause of failure, underachievement and settling for mediocrity.

The central and powerful message of this long and detailed conversation at the door was, "you can have and be anything you want to if you choose to believe. Also, every person on earth is blessed with the same power and ability if they choose to exercise it."

Hundreds of examples in my own life and the lives of those I've known flashed through my mind as this truth sank deeper and deeper into the fibers of my being. In a way that only can happen in this kind of a conversation, it seemed like thousands upon thousands of learnings, truths, and examples were laid out before my mind in an incredibly short period.

I grew more and more excited, partly for myself, but mostly at the thought of what a revolution the universal application of this truth would bring.

However, then I said, "This truth is already taught, and already widely known and doubted. Volumes have been written by famous and powerful authors trying to emphasize this awesome reality. What am I going to do to complete the work you have for me to improve and increase the power and effectiveness of this truth?"

I directed my mind back to a revelation I had been given earlier. I cannot affect everyone. I cannot even hope to affect a small fraction of those who live on the earth.

My work and my assignment in the agreement to remain on Earth is to do everything I can, as an example, teacher, and catalyst, so that every opportunity is maximized to increase the freedom, prosperity, and joy in the world that this principle provides.

Trembling at the magnitude of the assignment, even in my limited sphere, yet thrilled at the excitement provided by all the examples, I wondered what I could bring to the table to make this happen.

My assignment is to be a loud and clear voice about the capabilities inherent in each divine being. It is to trumpet from the mountaintops, in my writings, speeches, music, workshops, and every other venue, this truth, without fear, without apology, and without hesitation.

Inside, I yearned for some way to describe this, teach this and to lay it out differently than had ever been done before.

Knowing my thoughts, God gave me a revelation and framework to use, not only to increase awareness, but to grow the application of this fundamental truth: if you believe, and then act on those beliefs; you can create.

It's so simple when you think it through. Belief underpins every action. A farmer would not plant if he didn't believe in the harvest. An artist would not paint if they didn't believe in a finished painting.

A builder would not build if they didn't believe in the beautiful vision in the blueprints. We would not study if we didn't think we could learn. We would not practice a skill or an instrument or anything if we didn't believe we could get better.

Belief is the foundation. It drives assumptions, and then it drives actions, and actions drive results. The bigger the belief, the bigger the possibility. However, it all starts with belief.

As I groped in my mind for a way to formulate this powerful truth in a way that I could remember and use, suddenly a framework was laid out before my eyes.

The substance of that teaching is not the subject of this book. It requires a book of its own. It will be forthcoming in a book specifically dedicated to that framework and the power and opportunity that exists for every child of God.

I named that book, *The Book of Context*. Context was the word given to me to describe the limits that our beliefs impose on what we do, what we create, and therefore what we achieve.

It was laid out clearly and wholly and powerfully. My soul rejoiced at the clarity and power. My mind relaxed at the ease and simplicity of remembering this priceless gem.

Days later, the first thing I said to Joy upon being revived was a garbled and confusing explanation of this new book. I was barely coherent, but I remember the words tumbling from my lips and the excitement about the power, freedom, and prosperity this could create.

Back in the conversation with God, I continued by expressing overwhelming gratitude and excitement about the revelation that had come to mind. I was so excited I could barely contain myself.

We talked about how I could use this knowledge to bless and serve all of those around me. We talked about different ways that I could apply this principle to the benefit and assistance of everyone.

I expressed feelings of trepidation and being somewhat daunted at the magnitude of the task. Reassurance flooded my heart, and my soul as God reminded me repeatedly that He would be with me with guidance, information, and inspiration as required.

After all, this was my assignment from Him, and he would help me succeed as I diligently worked to make this real.

Again, I felt all the old desire that I had for the traditional markers of success and notoriety evaporate in the spirit of this conversation. The meaning of money, possessions, status, prestige, recognition, and all of the old symbols that had once been so important just vanished.

That's not to say we don't need to eat or live somewhere or take care of ourselves and those who depend on us. Instead, it was a fundamental shift in relative importance, and thus the focus and time and energy spent on the acquisition and display of such trivialities.

My mind and spirit were consumed by the visions and opportunities that lay before me. Peace, tranquility, and divine excitement fueled my heart and soul.

I was repeatedly struck by the complete difference between these conversations and all the other experiences I had while sedated. On the one hand was peace, love, and joy and the other was of turmoil, fear and blackness.

Other than a couple of hours for my gallbladder operation, or laser stapedotemy in my ears, or the restart on my heart following atrial fibrillation, I haven't been sedated, so I don't have any idea what people know or feel in such a time. For me, there were two distinct experiences.

These conversations at the door, and everything else.

All the conversations were bright, peaceful, full of light, hope, and love. The entire framework was one of kindness, forgiveness, moving forward, and adding good to the world. Everything else during my time of sedation was emptiness, terror, anxiety and colored either grey or black.

The conversation ended, and once again I was left to myself to ponder the blessing and commission I had been given and committed to accomplish.

The light stayed with me long enough to go through *The Book of Context* several times and anchor it with clarity in my thinking and consider the opportunities.

The time passed, and I was back in the grey emptiness.

Chapter 15

The Third Conversation at the Door

Another day passed, and I found myself again at the door to eternity. Things looked exactly as they had before, and I was in conversation with the same Divine Being.

I have no idea why I knew it was a day later; I only knew that it was. I imagined in my mind that it was time allowed for the previous conversations, choices, and commitments, to sink in.

Before the conversation even started, I was buzzing with excitement and expectation. The learning and power of the revelation from the day before hung heavily in the air. None of the previous conversations was repeated

Once the decision to stay was made, it was not discussed again. Once the truths were revealed, and the assignment given and agreed to, it also was not discussed again. I guess in the economy of God, once is enough.

Like the first conversation, this entire meeting was framed around one question. The question shocked me into silence and deep contemplation.

I waited, and the simple question startled me into silence. "Are you sure?"

The thought hung in the air in a kind, loving, gentle way. The implications penetrated me to the core. Doubt caused me to worry and to wonder.

Did I have any idea what I was getting myself into?

Was my commitment inadequate?

Had I missed something important?

Was the application and implementation of my work for God going to be so tough that I would wish that I had answered the first question differently?

I had absolutely no idea what to say, so I sat in silence for a long time, contemplating the different questions that had flooded my mind.

I thought through each possible interpretation to see what feelings arose and what I might've missed. Knowing that God would read my thoughts, I didn't speak any of this aloud.

The question that sat like a rock in my chest was: "Was getting in way over my head and not smart enough to know it?

Given the kindness and love which surrounded all three conversations, I knew that God was not setting me up for failure. I knew that if I were faithful, true and diligent that even if I made mistakes, His support would be there for me in more than enough measure to make it as it should be.

Given my pile of weakness and failings, I knew I would need help, but my previous experiences with prayer and meditation told me that support was available and that I would not be left alone.

After careful consideration, I decided that I know enough about what was coming and expected, and I knew enough about how to get the help that this would be okay.

Then I thought about whether or not I had missed something important. I thought about *The Book of Context*, and the rest of the framework that I would write to carry the message.

I thought about all the possible applications. At least all that was within my ability to conceive. I became painfully aware that there were undoubtedly dozens or even hundreds of situations and circumstances that were beyond my comprehension.

Again, I was assured through my faith and confidence in God that the conversation the day before would not have ended without covering all the crucial points.

This led me to an important truth that would be part of the framework. Often, we start on a path that intuitively we know is right, without knowing the end, and without even knowing much beyond the following step.

This is where the power of belief is manifest. We will often need to move forward right up to the edge of understanding, and then take a few steps into the dark, before clarity occurs about precisely what to do. This is the proverbial leap of faith.

The next angle I considered was whether my commitment was adequate. Like everyone else, I've had many times where I get excited about something, start with the project, and don't have the courage, the confidence or continuing reason to finish it.

The excuses are infinite and varied, and we all know how that feels. That is the last thing I wanted. I couldn't stand the thought that I had been blessed with such an experience, of being instructed by the divine, committing, and then somehow wavering in my resolve to see it through.

My commitment is solid. The instructions are clear. The things I value in life have changed, and I know without question in whom I have trusted and where to find power and comfort when I need it. This would not cause any doubt.

The final question caused some concern. Would the execution of this assignment be so complicated that I might waver or give up?

I thought about the number of times in my life that I had been selfish, a drug addict, failed others and been dishonest or undependable.

There were many times when I had worried more about what others thought of me than what I knew to be real or relevant. There were times when I had chased fame and fortune more than truth.

The whole first volume of the *TightRope of Depression* trilogy is littered with examples of failure, weakness, and callous behavior.

Was I indeed in a place where I was developed enough or could develop along the way to be sure about my commitment in this most serious and solemn of situations?

Surprisingly, this sobering line of thinking was not discouraging. It was an invitation to be *truthful to the core* and to be clear about whom I was talking to and what I was learning and saying.

The final answer came not for my wisdom, but from my confidence in the grace, truth, and love of God. I must trust that this had occurred at this time because it was the thing that needed to happen now. I had to trust that God would not send me on a mission to crash and burn.

My confidence was not in myself but Him.

Considering everything that had happened in my life, his willingness to forgive me and bless those I had hurt and given the fact that He had given me this assignment at this time, I was at peace. I experienced an upwelling of confidence, reverence, and overwhelming love.

Without question, I knew this was a fundamental turning point, and that living this truth and helping others understand and live their divine potential was my calling from this moment forward.

Then I spoke and said, "Yes, I'm sure."

There was an overwhelming feeling of love and support. We don't have the language to describe such feelings, but they are real and incomprehensibly powerful. I don't know how long they hung in the air, and I merely stood silently in the presence of the Almighty.

Time doesn't mean very much in that circumstance.

After a space of time, it was finished, and the conversation ended.

I was left to contemplate the singularity of the blessing I had received over the previous three days. I carefully reviewed all that I had seen, everything I had felt and the frameworks and principles that I'd been given.

I wanted fiercely to make sure that somehow, I forgot nothing and that everything would be preserved precisely as it was received.

Since I am writing this book now, and *The Book of Context* later, I choose to exercise faith and trust that I will recall whatever I need to remember.

Somehow, I knew that the interviews were finished. The last conversation ended with a sense of finality that let me know that the adventure had begun.

In reflection now, I note at the absence of questions and concerns that previously would have bothered me significantly.

"What will others think?"

"What if nobody believes anything I'm saying?"

"What if people think I'm completely crazy?"

"What if I fail?"

All those questions would previously have been a large part of my considerations. However, neither at the time of the interviews nor any time since have they even crossed my mind.

It is only now, as I sit here writing that I'm joyfully surprised at their absence. It's one more proof of the truth and power of the experiences I had at the door.

Part III – My Message, Your Mission

The *Mission: Impossible* series that has been on television in a couple of iterations over many years always starts with the head of the "Impossible Mission Force," getting a dossier and an assignment.

In the accompanying recording, whoever it is, and you never find out whom the voice belongs to, says "your mission, should you decide to accept it, is ..."

That's where we are in this story. I had an amazing experience. One I never imagined would come to me. An experience so powerful I was utterly overwhelmed, and at the same time, profoundly grateful.

In that experience, I received both a message and a mission. The message is that we have a loving and powerful creator. Because of that, each of us has a divine origin, infinite possibility and the availability of all the help we need to create any life we want.

My mission is to:

- Spread that truth to as many people as I can.

- Help them understand it to the core.

- If they want assistance, help them make it real in their lives.

Your mission, should you decide to accept it, is to investigate deep in yourself what you are doing with your life. The clock ticks by without delay and mercy. You have the opportunity to create anything you want, but the moments pass only once.

It is one thing to read a story about something that happened, then move back into our lives with no changes. It is quite another to allow a powerful message to drive us to create significant alterations.

I have already seen this message affect the lives of those I am working with. Surprising occurrences, interesting twists and fantastic changes have already taken place.

Action gives access to every power. This is a section of action. All dreams eventually end. My time in visits to the boundary between worlds also had an end.

No matter how glorious the message, there comes the time of execution. No message matters until it makes the difference it is designed to create.

Someone once defined the word "meaning" this way: The meaning of something is the difference it makes. If it makes no difference, it has no meaning.

The real story and value that this might create is the change in me and others because of my experience "at the door."

Waking up twice, as it were. First, spiritually through the experiences I had. Second, physically as I was brought back to consciousness in the ICU to see strange surroundings and people.

I told various medical personnel I had spoken with God and had experienced a near-death visitation, including being at the doorway, seeing the light and having conversations.

It mildly occurred to me they might think I was crazy, but I knew what was true and I didn't care.

The intensity of my descriptions had an impact. When I left the ICU a week later, the head physician, who had overseen the work of saving my life came in to wish me well.

He told me "I hope I never see you again," and smiled. Then, in earnest, he said: "but I want you to come back and tell me what you saw." I told him I would, and I meant it.

Another reason for writing this book.

Though the conversations with God at the doorway into eternity were concluded, the miracles were not finished. During the following weeks, I thought often and deeply about what happened and what it meant for the rest of my life.

I had no idea that there was more to come. The miracles have just begun.

Chapter 16

Day 20-25

University of Alberta Hospital ICU

It would be easy to think, "OK, the story is over, who cares about what else happened?"

Miracles come in many ways. One was that my life was preserved. Another was that I had this experience with God. A third is what happened and continues to happen as the consequences of this experience play out in my life.

A fourth will be those who make profound changes in their expectations and lives because they heed the call and seize the opportunity to alter the course of their futures dramatically.

In that spirit, I tell the next part of the story.

The next six days passed with the agonizing sluggishness of a bad B-movie. Each day seemed like three, and I swore the clock on the wall ran backward at times.

I didn't know anything about how long I had been unconscious until much later. I became aware of my surroundings again about June 23rd.

Of course, I only knew what day it was because somebody told me. After that, one of the questions each day was "what day is it?" I imagined that a correct answer meant I was still sane and making progress, so I struggled mightily to keep track of day and night.

From where I lay in the room there were no external cues about the passing of time and so the only way I kept track of it was by counting nights. A nurse turned out the lights, there was a long period with fewer people in the room, and the clock ran slower when I was supposed to be sleeping.

Anyone who has been in the hospital for an extended period knows how ridiculous it is to try to get good sleep. It may be the bed, the mattress, the tubes, the regular check of vital signs, the aching at pressure points where your body meets the bed or a host of other reasons.

I felt like I was awake all the time and that the world had slowed to a crawl. The only way to tell the story is to describe the significant things that made a difference.

Joy's visits

The highlight of every day was when Joy came. Because of her full attention during my period of unconsciousness, many things had been left untended at the house and in our personal circumstances. As soon as I gathered my wits about me, I told her to do what she needed to take care of herself, get the sleep she needed and care for our pets and the house as she saw fit.

Even so, she came every day between 9 and 10 am and stayed for two or three hours. She would update me on anything the doctors had told her about my condition. My recovery seemed slow, and generally, there was nothing to report.

She also kept me up to speed on the World Cup soccer matches which were in progress. I had a TV in my room and could watch if I wanted, but keeping my attention focused for long periods of time was very difficult.

I wasn't much of a soccer fan before Joy and I got married. She converted me to "fan status" for many international sporting events. The Tour de France, the World Cup and some other significant events that expanded my narrow "United States" myopia.

She would chatter about the teams that were in the running, her favorite players and the rights and wrongs of the referees in the previous days matches. I only followed about one-third of her explanations, but the chatter kept me occupied and did my mind good.

Besides the soccer matches and the information she could get from the doctors and nurses, she would tell me the antics with the animals and whatever else was going on in the house. Fortunately, we had a local place for doggy daycare, so our rambunctious puppy Cooper had a place to play every day while she was gone.

My vision without lenses is about 20/500 which is beyond the threshold of legal blindness. Without contacts, everything is a confusing blur. This added to my feeling of isolation and paranoia. Consequently, I wear very powerful contact lenses of a unique design.

The vision problems are because I have Keratoconus, which means the corneas of my eyeballs are mush. For many years I wore "piggyback" contact lenses. This is an arrangement with a nonprescription soft lens protecting the cornea and then a very steep and rigid hard lens on top to correct vision.

In the last year, these had been replaced by oversize lenses that go out to the whites of the eyeball. They are called scleral lenses, and they are complicated to put in and take out. Kind of like putting a pie plate in your eye.

Of course, that meant I couldn't do it by myself. One of the funnier and more tender pieces of this entire ordeal was Joy learning to put my contact lenses in and take them out because I couldn't.

The first time she put my lenses in it took about ½ an hour to get the first lens in my eye. The process is complicated, and you have to be at a precise angle, or they won't fit correctly.

Over and over again she tried, and the sheets got wet with contact lens fluid. It was funny and pathetic at the same time. I was determined to do whatever I needed to help her make it happen because I desperately wanted to see.

Eventually, she got the first lens in. The second one only took 15 minutes. After that, the insertion process got easier and easier until finally, the whole process took about five minutes for both lenses.

The time between her arrival and departure passed very quickly. After she left at 1 o'clock or so, I would swear the time slowed to a crawl and two days passed before she returned between 5 and 7 pm.

She would then stay till 9:30 or 10 pm when I would tell her to go home to get the sleep she needed to continue her superhuman effort at managing everything alone. Sometimes the routine varied a little here and there but not much. Those two periods were my highlight every single day.

Before she left in the evening, she would take out my contact lenses and of course that marked the end of my contact with the world and moved me into isolation and blindness once again.

As much as she had done during my period of complete sedation, she spared no effort at looking after my welfare. When I was too hot, she would talk to the nurses about temperature. Many times, she would go outside to get ice so I could have ice packs or wet towels to keep my temperature under control.

At the time, I had no idea what an ordeal it was to go in and out of my room. Later, having gone in and out of the door myself, I realized what she had been through each time I made a request. Because I was in biological isolation, she had to be suited up on arrival and wash up a certain way on departure.

<u>Nurses</u>

The nurses work 12-hour shifts. Most were female with a few male nurses on staff. They showed up first thing in the morning to take vitals. They introduced themselves and told me they were my nurse for the day. Each day we would go through a routine set of questions, I think to check my connection with reality.

"What day is today?" "Where are you?" "What is your name?" "Why are you here?"

These questions always happened first thing. I tried to keep track of the date and usually was within a day or two, but sometimes I just lost it and way off.

Every day they offered a sponge bath, a shave, and other personal care services. I skipped the shaving and decided to let the whiskers grow. Occasionally I took the sponge bath to stay clean.

All the tubes and devices connected to me made everything complicated. The catheter meant that I did not need to get up to use the bathroom. The nurses changed the feed bags, administered shots for pain and antibiotics and everything required to keep me healing.

I was amazed at how helpless I was. I have nothing but the utmost respect and admiration for those who do such work.

Other than me answering questions about why I was there, the subject of my illness and the status of my recovery were rarely discussed. I guess they wanted to keep me anxiety free. It had the opposite effect. I was desperate to understand the prognosis for recovery and healing.

I found the temperature of the room completely uncomfortable. I felt too hot all the time. I don't know if it was because I was feverish, the rooms were intentionally kept a bit on the warm side or because I like it cold. I requested cold towels and ice packs a lot.

The different personalities of the nurses were interesting. Some were very matter-of-fact and businesslike, and some were very accommodating with an entirely different bedside manner.

Sometimes during the nights, which were interminably long, I would hallucinate badly and begin making noises or calling out for help because I got confused or couldn't understand where I was.

It was then I got to see the significant differences between nurses. Some were patient with my periodic departure from reality, and others were abrupt in telling me to calm down.

Patient, mostly calm, attentive and dedicated, these angels of mercy were a big part of my every day and every night experience. I am quite sure I was not the easiest patient they had.

Hallucinations

The most troubling part of my entire stay was the hallucinations and delusions. As I think back on things I absolutely thought were right, I am astounded by the rich and powerful nature of these visual, auditory and physical occurrences.

All my hallucinations were frightening and sometimes downright terrifying. None were positive in any way, shape or form. I don't know, but I imagine the scary content came from being helpless in the hospital, combined with having depression for 45 years.

I regularly hallucinated about the room. It changed shapes and sizes. The windows were different. The decorations were different. These changes always felt unsettling and left me feeling off balance.

Once, there were Christmas decorations, and I was helping the nurse make them. I was standing up naked and complaining I didn't have everything I needed to finish the task. The nurse was ignoring me and busy stirring up something that looked like oatmeal. I think the "oatmeal" was the food that I was going to get through my feeding tube.

The nurse was suddenly gone, and I was left alone. It was snowing outside and a little bit inside. As I said earlier, I was naked and without a blanket or clothing. I was sure I was going to freeze to death and that this would be the way that I would die and not from MRSA or pneumonia.

Perhaps to compensate for my blindness, my hearing seemed sharpened to the point of madness. I could hear voices and whispering at all times. I became convinced that there was an investigation of my life going on.

Having been a drug addict in the past, I was positive that somehow, I would be arrested and the Royal Canadian Mounted Police (RCMP) would be there to take me to jail when my stay in the hospital was over.

A hallucination that continued day after day was of an imaginary person was sending me messages about herbal potions and concoctions that would ease my pain. I would draw the letters and words in the air so that this person could understand me and provide the appropriate mixture. Their answers appeared in writing I could see on the wall.

This became so real I imagined I had ordered some concoction for delivery and needed to pay a PayPal invoice. I remember talking to Joy about this purchase and asking her if she could handle the payment for me. Of course, there was no such invoice.

In one particularly vivid scene, I ordered supplements to make me stronger, like the blood additives that cause doping scandals in the sports world. In a lengthy conversation with this imaginary person, I specified the mixture, and they assured me they had it in stock.

The delivery of the potion was through a misting system in the room. The air would fill with mist, and I would be strengthened by its presence. I could see the mist; Joy could see nothing. I was convinced that she was just not looking. Again, it was frightening because I was part of a world that no one else could see.

One unusually long and miserable night, I imagined that one of the nurses was giving me more pain medication than I wanted. I kept refusing, and she injected me with it anyway. When the nurse was out of the room, I frantically wrote a message to my imaginary potion master, asking them to intervene somehow and report this extra pain medication.

Nothing happened, and no rescue came. I knew it was proof of conspiracy. I imagined that the pain medication was being given because I made too much noise and the nurse wanted me quiet. None of it was real.

The doctors told Joy later that such delusions are common, especially for someone who's been in isolation as long as I was, and they can at times be problematic. At least this way she knew what was going on.

Another hallucination showed up as an exaggeration of things that were really happening. Shots, feeding tubes, and other routine procedures became exaggerated and strange.

As part of the paranoia, I saw sensors growing out of the ceiling in different places in the room. I knew for sure that there were cameras and microphones in those sensors which were spying on me and recorded everything that I said and did.

I became terrified that in my sleep I was going to say something that would somehow be twisted in an incriminating way to strengthen the case waiting for me if I ever got healed. I created incredible stories about the sensors that showed up regularly all over the room.

They popped out of the ceiling in the same place every day and tentacles came out to get close to me to record vital signs, breathing cadences and everything about my movements and thoughts. Every hour I was alone was filled with one terror or another. This meant that my waking time was filled with such anxiety that sleep was difficult and frightening.

The paranoia about investigation and examination even extended to my house. I "remembered" that on being admitted to the hospital I signed something that gave away privacy rights on the pretext that it was necessary for treatment.

I imagined this included invading computers, music, and writings at home, and everything else. All designed to work against me. I struggled to think of anything that was in my house or on my computers that would connect to my incriminating past.

On reflection, and with the understanding that anxiety and depression are natural side effects of sedation, I expect that the persecution complex came from my lifelong battle with depression and not feeling "good enough."

The hallucinations, fear, and anxiety were the worst part of my stay in the hospital.

Feeding Tubes

In sedation, any nourishment has to come intravenously. When the two weeks of sedation was completed, they continued feeding me through a feeding tube. If you've never had one, it is an experience you can forego your whole life without missing anything.

It normally wouldn't be worth mentioning in a book like this, but the drama around my feeding tube was a major ordeal. Shortly after I came out of the coma, we tried to insert a feeding tube. They go up your nose, down your throat and into the stomach.

This first attempt was a complete disaster. It was excruciating. I was also hallucinating at the time and, while I tried my very best to be accommodating and follow instructions, I could not swallow the device as instructed.

I felt like the nurse was insensitive and cruel. She did not understand how hard I was trying and how bad the whole procedure seemed to hurt. She abandoned the attempt and left the room.

I lay there softly weeping partly from pain, partly from frustration and partly from failing to try hard enough to get the tube inside. I'm sure it was all wildly exaggerated because of my condition.

She came back later and asked what the matter was. I told her she was unkind and that I had been doing my best to make this all work. Things calmed down, and a bit later a different nurse came in to try again. I gathered my courage, expecting another disaster, and prepared for the ordeal.

Somehow, this time I swallowed at just the right moment and the tube went down my esophagus and into my stomach. Victory at last. Just having the tube in your nose down your throat and in your stomach 24 hours a day is not much fun. You are always aware of its presence.

Every time they start a new bag of food you can feel it appearing in your stomach without having done the work of chewing and swallowing. It is particularly unnerving when they flush the food with water to keep you hydrated. It feels like I suddenly drank a glass of water with no effort.

They also administered one of the antibiotics this way. That was weird because it had a peculiar flavor which lingered for ½ an hour or so.

One day after the tube was successfully inserted, it stopped working. They tried different ways to get it working again to no avail. Eventually, they had to pull it out. Somehow, it had kinked and failed. I was horrified at the prospect of doing this over again.

An hour later, someone came in to do it all over again. This was my third time through the ordeal. I knew what to expect regarding pain and where it would hurt. My experience let me swallow it just a little quicker, making this process slightly less traumatic.

Imagine my horror on finding that this tube also failed after one day. It was no longer passing the food into my stomach, and the bags were not draining. Once again, they pulled the tube out, which is an experience by itself. A couple of hours later, for the fourth time, we inserted a tube in my nose and into my stomach.

Gratefully, this one worked for several days. Eventually, it too failed. By the fifth time, it had become less traumatic; I guess practice makes perfect.

The fact that this happened five times is the reason I mention it at all. I can't imagine why in the world it was my joy and blessing to have that happen, but it was.

Part of the story.

Trying to Walk

On the second or third day after I regained consciousness, a physical therapist (PT) came to see me. He was a friendly fellow and said something I was utterly unprepared to hear.

"Let's see if you can walk." I tried to move my leg to the edge of the bed and onto the floor. It would not budge, and I had to physically reach down with my hands and pull it over the side of the bed.

An auspicious beginning to my new world of walking. Joy was there for this first attempt, so she got to participate in the process. The therapist, a nurse, and Joy all helped me sit up and scoot to the edge of the bed.

The PT brought over something that looked like a tackling dummy with no padding on wheels. He told me to stand up, which of course was a joke all by itself. It slowly dawned on me that I had no physical strength whatsoever. I looked at my legs and saw that they had shrunk to the size of toothpicks.

Joy found later in her research online that a sedated body loses up to 2% of its muscle mass per day of unconsciousness. Great, that meant 30% of my muscle mass was history.

They strapped a 6-inch wide belt around me, and with the combined efforts of three people and my weak contribution, I managed to stand up while clutching the apparatus. Holding this device in a death grip, I managed to take a few steps toward the door. I was utterly exhausted and terrified at the idea that I was so broken.

I had a great desire to perform well, so I tried with all my might to walk with some semblance of normalcy. I failed miserably and realized once again that I was helpless. I shuffled back toward the bed. Instead of getting in bed, the PT told me to sit in a chair. The goal was to sit upright for about 30 minutes.

After 10 minutes, I was extremely fatigued and asked to lay down. Joy played her part as the tough coach and kept me sitting. She watched a soccer match and ignored my frequent protests until the time had passed. I gratefully staggered into my uncomfortable bed, realizing how much better that was than either sitting or trying to walk.

The next day we did the same thing. I was joyfully surprised when I was able to not only make it to the door but through the double doors and out into the hallway.

This was my first glimpse of the place I had been captive for 2½ weeks. Still tightly clutching my mobile pillar, breathing heavily and moving tentatively, I made it all the way down the hall.

Resting for a moment in a chair, I then made my way back. I was exultant at the progress of just one day. To my great consternation, I was again supposed to sit upright for half an hour. I was sure this would not go well. After 10 or 15 minutes it became difficult, and the fatigue was overwhelming, but with Joy's encouragement, I made it through and then collapsed back into bed.

Two days later, a third PT came for my walk. This time, we made it down the hallway twice. I doubled the distance that I was able to walk. I began to have hope that this wouldn't take forever.

Two days after that, another PT came to help me with my walk. This time we exited the ICU and walked down the hallway in the main part of the hospital.

For the first time, I realized that the area where I was being treated was completely isolated from the rest of the hospital even though it was in the same building. I saw that the air system and the entrance were all separated from the main structure. It gave new meaning to the term "isolation."

Once again, I was ecstatic that we had extended the walk much further. I was positively winded and trembling when we got done, but that was okay because I got back in one piece and had done the distance.

The increasing success of these walks was the first piece of hope that I had, other than breathing and being alive, since I had regained consciousness.

Clearing My Lungs

Severe pneumonia in both lungs creates fluid, mucus, scar tissue and dying bacteria which have to be cleaned out to get healthy.

Right after getting off the bronchial tubes, which go down the throat, but before I regained consciousness, they inserted a tracheal tube so they would have direct access to my lungs through my neck.

Between two and four times a day, the nurse would administer something called a "puffer." The purpose of this process is to get me to cough all the accumulated filth up the trachea to remove it from the lungs.

The stuff they put in your lungs to make you cough is the most awful, foul-smelling substance imaginable. In my worst nightmares, no sewer gas, dying carcass or anything I have ever smelled was so horrific. I can't even conceive of anything that smelled worse.

Instantly, it has the desired effect. The gas is inserted into your lungs, and even though I have no idea how this works, it feels like you're smelling it, tasting it and experiencing it viscerally all at the same time.

Immediately I coughed repeatedly and violently and expelled copious quantities of awful filth from my lungs. As I coughed, my eyes would close. With each cough, I saw a different color before my eyes.

It was like looking through one of those Kaleidoscopes as a kid, except that the background was black instead of white and the colors seemed neon bright.

I vaguely heard the nurse congratulating me on how much of the awful stuff I had expelled. Knowing the purpose of this, I obliged and coughed as much as I could. After this happens, they put in three or four puffs of an inhaler to expand the bronchial tubes and improve breathing.

To start with, I dreaded it when the nurse came in with that device. As the days went on, I realized it was making me breathe better. I began asking for its application whenever I found myself struggling to breathe. As the days wore on, less and less came up from the lungs, and they started talking about removing the trachea tube from my throat. I was excited.

Progress.

Getting Ready to Move

The day finally came that they took the tube out of my throat. They closed the hole and gave me instructions that the next few days when I coughed I needed to put my finger on the spot where the hole was, so I wouldn't blow out the closure.

The conversation then began about when I might move from ICU up to the regular hospital ward. I started asking in earnest what had to happen for me to make the move. I didn't want to spend the rest of my life in the ICU.

Even though I had completed three walks down the hall, with the last one being out into the regular hospital, I was still seriously in need of a walker. My steps were slow, and my breathing was labored. With the trachea tube removed and my lungs cleared out enough so we no longer needed the smelly puffer from hell, it was clear that I could be cared for in a regular ward.

Finally, the joyous day came. It was not as ceremonious an event for them as it felt for me since moving people around to different places in the hospital was pretty standard.

For me, it was a big deal.

It meant progress. I was on the road to recovery. Based on the conversations I heard, I expected that there would be at least three more weeks in the recovery ward before we could even talk about going home.

On the last day in ICU, a respiratory therapist (RT) had come in to test my breathing. It was still shallow and weak, but the terrible coughing fits were smaller, and the verdict was that it was time to leave the joys of the ICU behind.

They took out the last IVs. Good thing, because it was getting hard to find places to put them. Several veins had collapsed because the IV had been inserted for so long.

I was put on a different bed and wheeled out of the ICU for the last time. Down the hall to the elevator and back up to the fifth floor. Same floor where I started the adventure, three weeks before.

Chapter 17

Day 26 – 30

University of Alberta Hospital Ward

You never know how things will twist and turn. This part of the story, starting after the ICU, is essential because of the incredible miracle which took place a few days later. It all seems like normal hospital routine, but it was a path leading to another astonishing milestone in this unbelievable journey.

I was so excited to get out of the ICU and into the regular part of the hospital. On the day we moved I didn't care how many weeks I had left, it was just better to be making progress.

My trachea tube was out. The scar was healing so pretty soon I wouldn't have to put my finger on the hole when I coughed or talked. I didn't have to endure that horrific smelling gas to make me cough anymore. There were so many things that just felt better.

On top of that, my room had a window, and I could see outside. Well, sort of outside. The central part of the hospital had a big skylight above the top floor, and daylight came into a large atrium. My window opened on that atrium. Now I could tell when it was daylight and dark and not be confused about the passing of days.

My door was open, and I could see the nurse station outside. I could see people walking by regularly and suddenly isolation was reduced. I was very excited. I was still in a private room, in semi-isolation, and all staff and visitors had to mask, glove, and gown up before entering my room.

On the other hand, I was still hooked up to a catheter. I could barely walk 30 meters without becoming winded and in desperate need of a chair. I was also starving to death, or at least it felt like it.

Every time I looked at my body, I could see that my limbs had shriveled up, but the staff assured me this was normal and nothing surprising.

The number of visits from therapists and doctors in different specialties was increasing. This meant we were focusing on recovery. I can't remember them all, but the main focus was physical therapy and respiratory therapy.

Trying to Breathe

Coming off severe pneumonia in both lungs and having been on life support for two weeks, the respiratory resident was concerned about lung functionality, capacity, and healing. My initial breathing performance was abysmal.

I coughed severely at the smallest attempt of a deep breath. I felt that what I could produce when told to take a deep breath and blow out as hard as I could, was astonishingly small.

I got something that looked like a toy. It was a small plastic apparatus with a little yellow disc inside. The instructions were to inhale in a fashion that held the disc in suspension between the top and the bottom space in the apparatus.

I was told to do these exercises 100 times, three or four times a day. Having nothing to do, I must've done it a thousand times the first day. Somehow, I thought if I were extra diligent in doing these exercises somebody would be impressed. They weren't.

It wasn't that difficult to keep the disc in the middle, but if I breathed very deeply while I kept it in the middle, I would immediately fly into a coughing spasm. The nurse said this was normal and not to worry. Just go right ahead and cough and keep on practicing.

I think I did the exercise 10,000 times over the next few days. I don't know if that helped overall. Just one more piece of the puzzle. I was still on oxygen. I had this discouraging vision of dragging around an oxygen tank at age 62 when I finally did get out of the hospital.

Over the next three days, they gradually lowered the percentage of oxygen and then it was removed entirely, meaning I was breathing entirely on my own. I noticed and felt the loss of oxygen because my breathing exercises became more difficult. I guess if my overall saturation levels were adequate I would take that as progress.

Thinking About the Books

Besides wondering about how long the recovery would take, my mind was also busy with what had happened during my visits with God at the boundary between life and eternity. Over and over again I went through the conversations in detail. I was overwhelmed by the astonishing fact that they occurred at all.

So much of what happened in the hospital was hazy and difficult to remember. The conversations were clear, detailed and easy to recall.

I briefly wondered what would've happened if I had chosen to go home to God instead of staying here. I quickly decided that it didn't matter because I did decide to stay, and my agreements about the future were clear.

I repeatedly talked to Joy about what happened, what I learned and what it would mean for my work and my purpose when I eventually got home. She was excited and supportive.

I also spent hours thinking about *The Book of Context*. This was the name of the book that would house the principles that I had learned about taking control of life and creating it precisely the way you want it to be.

I began formulating the principles I had learned into a framework that I could use in coaching and mentoring those clients that I am blessed to work with.

I also began thinking about how to apply this to every aspect of life. Not just work life, but everything. I realized that it could work for anything and everything that anyone chooses to accomplish.

I got some paper and tried to take notes. That was a futile effort because my hands were so shaky that I couldn't read what I wrote even at the time. This one was of those times where you think you're more capable than you are.

I saved one of those note pages, and I still can't make out what I was trying to write. I'm grateful that my memories are so detailed and vivid.

The Book of Context is being written at the same time as this volume. Information about that book and guidance about how to benefit are contained at the end of this book.

My mind was certainly healing faster than my body. I was eager and anxious to start fulfilling the commitments I had made by writing and sharing what I had learned.

Two problems interfered with my thinking and made my life in a hospital bed still uncomfortable and frightening.

Hallucinations

One thing that did not change at all in my move from the ICU to the regular hospital ward was the hallucinations; they continued unabated.

It is difficult to describe how powerful and threatening these images felt. I still saw antennas and receivers growing out of the ceiling. These were receivers tied to spy devices that were somehow monitoring my thoughts.

They were so real and frightening that I would try to point them out to Joy when she was there. She was patient and kind with my delusions.

At first, she merely said she could not see them and that they were not real. After a time, she had conversations with the medical staff and learned that this might go on for several weeks. Staff also told her that they should gradually diminish and disappear with time.

Sometimes she took a more active approach by trying to help me understand that they were not real and that I was making all of this up. I wanted to accept what she was telling me, but the reality of the hallucinations was so powerful, during the daylight and even with her presence that I could not "un-see" what I was staring at in real time.

When Joy was gone, my newly "sharpened hearing," overheard conversations by medical staff in the hallway where they were blackmailing former patients with the information they had gathered with just such devices.

I "heard" very clearly conversations both on the phone and with people that I thought I saw in person, who were negotiating deals about what their monthly blackmail payment would be to maintain the silence of the staff.

In retrospect, it all sounds ridiculous. At the time it was real, powerful and horrifying.

I "remembered," conversations that didn't occur, even to the point of imagining that I had confronted the head resident with these conspiracies and he had just brushed me off. That made me believe that the entire hospital staff was part of a grand extortion scheme.

One of the most persistent and terrifying hallucinations revolved around the clock.

For some reason, the clock on my wall wasn't normal and didn't mark the passage of time as it should. The numbers slid around the clock face, and after an hour would pass somehow the numbers had moved so that it only showed the passage of a few minutes.

This magnified the sense that something was wrong and that I was going to be a prisoner there forever. During times I was not hallucinating, I stared at the clock intently to verify what I was seeing, but I could never focus on it sufficiently to gain clarity.

After three days, the clock face looked completely different. I would've sworn that the staff had changed the clock and that a new apparatus was now hanging on the wall. Unlikely, but that is what I saw. The frequency and intensity of these hallucinations fueled the other feeling that made the hospital stay challenging.

<u>Anxiety</u>

At least seven or eight times a day, I found myself overwhelmed with the feeling of anxiety. I guess you could call them panic attacks. This created an unnerving fear that gripped my heart. I have never been prone to anxiety attacks or severe nervousness. I have had Major Depressive Disorder (MDD) since I was in my teens.

I know that anxiety often goes with depression, but this had not been part of my pathology. However, it was in full power as I lay in the hospital bed. I lay awake deep into the night, getting very little sleep because of the conversations that I was imagining.

One night, I saw that everything outside of my room was under construction. This continued late into the night. The door to my room had was closed so I could sleep. I got up and knocked on my own door at 2:30 am to ask the resident who answered if it was okay to use the washroom. I could see light under the door, and I thought someone was using it.

The doctor assured me that it was a private restroom for my use only. The light was left on so that I could find it. My mind had reconfigured the doorways, and I imagined a door that led from the bathroom out to the public hallway.

Joy

Just as it had been in ICU, the best part of every day was Joy's visits. She had about the same schedule, arriving at 9 am and staying until 11 am or sometimes until lunch, then returning in the evening for a few more hours.

Of course, she got to eat, while I was still being fed "imaginary food" through the nose tube. This fifth tube had managed to last and didn't fail. Joy insisted they increase the amount of food I was getting, and they agreed. I got an extra bag of protein-rich food every day.

I craved her visits because they provided several things. First, I got my contact lenses in, so I could connect with the world. Second, it was my chance to ask her if any of the imaginary stuff I was seeing and hearing could be real. Of course, it wasn't. I marvel at her patience as I think about how hard I tried to explain to her what she was missing.

She tried her best to help me understand what was real and what was made up. She helped me focus on her and what I had experienced with God and just to leave the rest alone. As long as she was there, I felt somehow safe from all the conspiracies, imaginary messages and everything else that my mind was creating.

Finally, I began to accept that these visions are at least somewhat common for people who had been through similar trauma. They became less threatening, and I relaxed a bit.

Starving

Since starting physical therapy by trying to walk, first with the pillar on wheels and then with a walker, I felt the reality of the atrophy of my body. Besides looking ridiculously thin and having lost an undetermined amount of weight, I was so weak that every movement, even in bed required considerable effort. On top of that, I felt like I was starving to death.

I began to pester the staff about when I could eat regular food. I assumed that if I could eat regular food, then I could have enough to satisfy my hunger.

I was told that I couldn't have anything in my mouth until I had a "swallowing test." I hadn't taken anything by mouth for nearly a month, and they couldn't risk aspiration into the lungs until this test was complete.

This conversation started the day I got up onto the ward. They told me that the swallowing test might happen the next day. They had to check the schedule. I came to the ward on Friday. The next day was Saturday, and so the news came back that it was possible but unlikely. Perhaps Sunday.

Unfortunately, Sunday morning at 2:30 am, during restless attempts to sleep, my fingers got tangled up in the feeding tube which came out of my nose and over the top of my head. I pulled the tube out about an inch or so which jolted me to full consciousness. At first, I thought I had been tangled in the oxygen tube, except the oxygen had been removed on Saturday night.

Then I realized I had partially pulled out the feeding tube. I panicked and did not know what to do. Should I cram it back in?

For some reason, I didn't think of ringing the emergency button for the nurse and getting help. It was the middle of the night, and I was in the full grip of anxiety and restlessness.

Feeling wholly frustrated and without recourse, I just pulled the tube out all the way and threw it across the room into the sink.

I then sank back in the bed, trying to get some sleep in all the madness. I took some small comfort in the fact that they had mentioned that I might get the swallowing test later today and be able to eat real food.

Sunday morning came, and the nurse saw the tube in the sink and asked what happened. I explained what had taken place and that I was hoping to have the swallowing test. I don't think she believed me. Her expression was one of exasperation.

I thought I overheard a discussion about whether or not to put another tube in my nose. I pleaded with them not to put me through that ordeal again, but instead get the swallowing test so I could eat.

They said they would check the schedule and see what they could do.

No answer came back for several hours. Then I was informed it was too late. It felt like I had gone most of the day without any nourishment. I'm sure it wasn't as long as I imagined.

They hooked me up to some glucose solution intravenously, and I went through the rest of the day in the forlorn hope that somehow Monday I could get the swallowing test.

Monday was a holiday. Sometime during the day, they told me that there was no staff to do the test and it would have to wait till Tuesday. Finally, Monday evening, the resident in charge of the floor told me on her way out that she had put notes in the file and promised me that no matter what, it would be first thing Tuesday morning.

It wasn't, and just like every other day, Tuesday morning started with no mention of any test. I was beginning to feel desperate.

Small Steps

In the midst of all this panic, there were a few bright spots. On Saturday, they removed the catheter, and I was allowed to go to the bathroom. It was embarrassing at first because someone was on the spot, helping me all the way.

After one attempt like that, I assured them that I thought I could manage alone. It was a lot harder than I expected, but I made it.

It was the same with the shower. On Saturday, I took a shower, clinging to the supports fastened to the walls. The nurse was there assisting me all the way through.

Normally, I would've been embarrassed, except I had been in the hospital long enough that any sense of propriety had long since evaporated. I was just grateful that I could have a real shower. I enjoyed standing in the warm water as long as I could before fatigue ended my reverie.

On Monday, I took a shower on my own. It took a really long time. I needed frequent pauses to catch my breath, but I managed. The long shower was good because it made another hour pass.

Another piece of good news was that I was finally able to stand up and use the walker on my own to get a little exercise. On both Sunday and Monday, I walked or rather hobbled outside my room, around the nursing station and back into my hideaway.

Monday I completed two circuits around the nursing station. There were about 15 rooms around the central work area. I saw people going in and out of these rooms. Things seemed almost like normal.

As I walked around, I could also see all the workstations and people busy with their jobs. I realized that I could not reconcile the hallucinations with what I was seeing. A tiny ray of hope began to shine. Perhaps all the terror I was hearing was not real after all.

What's the Plan?

The most challenging part of all this was the fact that I could not seem to get any information about what the measurements of recovery were. What constituted progress and success? Everything I had heard indicated that it would be 2 to 4 weeks before I would get out of the hospital and go home.

Physical therapists, respiratory therapists, and occupational therapists visited me on a daily basis for conversation about how I was feeling and some work in their specialty.

To my frustration, nothing was ever said about creating a timeframe for release. When I inquired, everyone was very vague about marking progress, only saying that there was still much work to do. I guess they were trying to keep my expectations low so that I wouldn't be surprised when the timeframe was long.

My frustration, anxiety and outright paranoia reached a peak on Tuesday when the nurse and then the therapist came in with no news about the swallowing test and acting like, despite the previous day's assurances from the head resident, it was unlikely that they would fit me in that day.

After all, Monday had been a holiday, and they were completely booked up. The glucose solution I was receiving felt inadequate. I felt like my body was evaporating.

Despite her persistence, Joy couldn't get any details from the medical staff either.

Chapter 18

The Miracle – Day 30

University of Alberta Hospital Ward

At about 11 am on Tuesday morning, July 3, at the peak of this anxiety, a thought penetrated my consciousness. It came so powerfully and urgently that I acted on it at once.

It came in the form of a question, which I immediately recognized as coming from a divine source. It felt like the conversations I had with God at the door.

"Why don't you apply the principles I gave for The Book of Context to this situation." This is precisely the meaning of creating your own life.

Without hesitation, I asked myself the following question. "What do I believe about this situation?" The answers came tumbling out of my mind, and I listed them quickly.

- I believe I will be here forever.

- I believe I can't find out what's going on.

- I believe I cannot change this.

- I believe no one is concerned about what I'm going through.

- I believe I am helpless.

- I believe it is hopeless for me to push for any change.

- I believe the overwhelming anxiety and fear will never leave.

- I believe there is nothing I can do about any of this.

All of this felt precisely true. I could get no information, I could not get the swallowing test even scheduled, and I had no idea about what the process was to get organized about my recovery.

The consequence of these beliefs was the intense anxiety and fear I was feeling. It was choking the life out of me. Perhaps it was even contributing to the intensity of my hallucinations.

The second question then welled up in my mind. "What else *could* I believe about this situation?" The answers came more slowly.

I *could* believe there is a way to get some information. I *could* believe that eventually I'll get this test scheduled and get on with it.

Immediately, the "voice of reason," interfered and started shouting in my ears. "That's ridiculous, you've asked several times, they promised several times, and nothing is happening. You can *make believe* that these things are possible, but you know it's not true."

I recognize this is the same old voice of doubt and fear that always accompanies any effort that we make to create a future that is not a repetition of the past.

I also recognize it as a prevailing attitude and affliction of clients and others I work with when faced with the possibility of change that is significant and challenges the status quo.

I used the skill I have developed over 45 years of meditation practice to set those thoughts aside and started once again to list the things I *could* believe.

- I *could* believe that these people are doing their best.

- I *could* believe that I will get the test sometime soon and get food.

- I *could* believe that there is a schedule somewhere about how many weeks I will be here and that eventually, I can have it.

- I *could* believe that it is difficult to put a schedule together because it depends on my progress.

- I *could* believe there is no neglect of my feelings.

- I *could* believe there is no need for anxiety and fear and then eliminate them.

- I *could* believe that all is well and be at peace.

After listing these possible beliefs and repeatedly eliminating the insistent negative chatter that is always present in such circumstances, I considered the consequences of such beliefs.

If I believed these things, I would be at peace. Whatever steps there were to healing, or whatever the number of weeks I would be in the hospital, they could pass in joy and growth.

I chose to accept these new beliefs and replace the old ones. I entered a state of meditation and focused with all of the intensity I could bring on creating this change.

Describing the process of this meditation and connecting to the raw power of the universe is beyond the scope of this book. I teach it in my work with clients. The foundation piece, however, is precisely a *choice* to change belief.

After 30 minutes of intense work, a feeling of peace swept over me, and I collapsed back into the uncomfortable hospital bed.

A few minutes later four people with clipboards walked into the room. Two of them immediately began moving my bed and maneuvering me toward the door.

"Where are we going?" The question tumbled from my lips in earnest curiosity. "We're going down to do the swallowing test," came the answer immediately.

No notice, no scheduling, merely an immediate response to my choice to change my context.

We rolled out in the hallway across the atrium and to the elevators on the other side. We went down to the second floor and to a place I had never been before, where this test will be conducted.

One other person was waiting for their test. I sat there for about 15 minutes and was then ushered into the testing chamber.

The test took about 30 minutes. An x-ray device was put up by my throat which allowed the technician and me to see all the inside workings in my neck. I could look at the bones and the outlines of the trachea and esophagus.

A fascinating sight. Different substances infused with barium would be put in my mouth so I could swallow them. The point was to visually observe the process and see if there was any danger of aspiration into my lungs.

The only scary part was when I was given a large dry cracker and told to chew it up and swallow it. I was worried that the tiny pieces might present a problem. They didn't.

I passed the test, and I asked the technician how long it would be before the information got up to the fifth floor that I could now eat. She assured me that I could take the test results with me.

I was wheeled back out in the hallway clutching my test results, waiting for the orderlies to come and take me back up to my room. I was excited. I was bummed at having missed lunch, but I was looking forward to some wonderful hospital food for dinner.

I was no sooner back in my room than a physical therapist came in. Because this is a University hospital, there are always many residents in training. This meant that nearly every resident I had seen was someone different. This time, I recognized this fellow from the ICU.

He said we were going to go do some walking and I figured "no big deal, I hobbled two full circuits with my walker around the nurse's station yesterday."

"You told us there were stairs in your house, is that correct?"

"Yes."

"Then we are going to need to do the stair test today."

"What is the stair test?"

"You have to climb ten stairs."

My heart beat fast, and my breath choked in my throat. I thought wildly "are you mad?" My mouth simply said, "sure, no problem."

Clutching my walker and trailing all my measurement gear, we hobbled our way past the entrance to the ward and into the hallway. Partway down was a door on the left.

We went through this giant industrial door and found ourselves in the stairwell. Now, this was a large industrial staircase like you see in a hospital. Go figure.

He looked at me and said, "Climb ten stairs."

I stared at him in disbelief and finally choked out the words, "Does it matter how I do this?"

"No, just climb ten stairs."

In my mind's eye could see myself crawling up ten stairs on my hands and knees. I figured that wouldn't do so I sidled up to the bottom stair and clutched the railing for dear life.

I then made my way slowly and with labored breathing up ten stairs. Pausing for a full minute to get my breath, I then made my way down again and stood there with a triumphant look on my face.

With my walker, I made my way back to my room and collapsed back into bed.

Less than five minutes later another fellow walked in. He asked me a question that I could not believe I heard.

"When do you want to go home?"

Assuming I was finally going to get a schedule of how many weeks were left and what the process would be to measure healing, I jokingly answered "Yesterminute."

He looked at me quizzically and repeated my word. "Yesterminute?"

Realizing that it could be confusing, I explained with a smile, "You know, yesterday, yester-hour, yester-minute."

It took 15 seconds for it to land and then he laughed appreciatively. He began to do some paperwork and I still was expecting a conversation about a lengthy process for rehabilitation to go home.

We exchanged some other small talk, and he left. Presently two nurses came in and asked about my belongings. Gradually it dawned on me.

I was going home, right now.

I had barely been out of the ICU five days. I had only been de-catheterized Saturday. I had taken one shower. I had not had one piece of solid food or anything in my mouth for a month.

Somehow, the process I had used from *The Book of Context*, and my intense connection to the creative power of the universe had manifested a miracle beyond my wildest understanding and expectation.

Without any preamble, I had created the situation that I could get out of the hospital, immediately.

I didn't know whether to be excited or terrified. Frankly I was both. I thought about my weakened condition and everything that would have to happen at home for me to even get by.

The nurses began asking about whether I needed to take a walker and what I might need in the way of rehabilitative support. They told me where I could get these things after I left the hospital and proceeded as if everything were completely moving as expected.

What was happening was so far from my expectation and everything I had been led to believe, I was still completely in shock. I was going home, NOW.

Impossible Miracle

In less than an hour, I was sitting in a wheelchair at the entrance to the University of Alberta Hospital, waiting for Joy to pull up, help me in the car and go home.

I wept, I pondered, and I could hardly comprehend what had just happened.

I knew with absolute certainty that this was a miracle created by the process I had used. I also knew that this miracle was given so that I could understand without question the awesome and staggering power available in this way.

I also realized that this was an integral part of the teaching and process that would be used as I wrote *The Book of Context*, and began to use it in both my coaching practice, in my own life and with those that I work with in other circumstances.

Joy could not believe what was happening either. Nothing she had heard or that had been discussed had prepared her for this turn of events.

We hugged. We laughed. We prayed. Then we drove home, almost. One stop before home – A&W to get a juicy hamburger and fries.

There is nothing more to say.

Chapter 19

Day 31 – The Present: Recovery & Home

As I got home, I felt a strange sense of arrival. I had come back to the house, surroundings, and circumstances I expected. I also felt as if I had come home to God.

I didn't know what the next days and weeks would bring. I only knew that this miracle had happened according to plan and that it all related to the conversations at the door.

I also knew that by no means were the miracles finished and that I had much more to learn and to do as I prepared myself for the commitments I had made.

Clutching the railing and making my way up the 16 stairs to our second-story bedroom, I wept tears of gratitude again, both for the miracle that had just happened and for the amazing journey of the previous 30 days.

My mind contemplated the seriousness of what had happened. I had a life-threatening illness. I had nearly died. I had been given another chance at life and a choice to take it. I had made choices and commitments.

I was overwhelmed by the pure joy at having been blessed with such an experience and the responsibility that I had undertaken.

Panting and out of breath, I sat on the bed looking at my wrists and arms. I was amazed at the marks and scars from the IVs that bore silent witness to the work that had taken place to save my life.

I expected to go to sleep, but sleep didn't come for some time, as I lay pondering what had happened during each part of the journey and meditating on what the unknown but glorious future would bring.

The Physical Part

There are three parts to the story of the first month of recovery – the Physical part, the Mental part, and the Spiritual part. I was repeatedly amazed at how atrophied my muscles had become. I was so weak I could barely walk to the bathroom, a distance of about ten feet.

I went straight to bed and stayed there till morning. Never before in my life had I so firmly believed that sleep is the best way for the body to repair itself.

Everyone knows you don't get any sleep in the hospital, but now I was a firm believer and absolute witness of that incontrovertible reality. My own bed felt wonderful.

The next day I got my first look in the mirror at what I had become. I looked like a walking scarecrow. My arms and thighs had shriveled up to toothpicks and when I came downstairs, my mother-in-law was horrified at the sight. The stooped posture and shuffling gait didn't help.

We all decided that I could qualify as an extra for a WWII prisoner of war movie. As funny as that sounds to say, it was not an attractive site, and I was certainly planning to do something about it. I had no idea what a challenge that would prove to be.

There had never been a time in my life when I could not get on the floor and do 40 push-ups. So I figured that my push-up count would be a good measure of how much I had deteriorated.

Later that day, I laid on the floor and began my push-ups. To my astonishment and dismay, I could not get my nose out of the carpet. Not one single push-up. Not even ½ of a push-up.

I was very disappointed and a little frightened. I had enjoyed fantastic health and an astoundingly sound physical constitution my whole life. Now it felt completely broken.

Over the next few days, I struggled as I tried to walk further and further. I have a Fitbit which tracks my steps, so, I was excited when I got to 500 steps in a day.

Then finally 1,000, which soon became 2,000, and 4000 and 6000. Eventually, I got to 10,000 steps in a day. On that day I completely wore out my body.

The biggest barrier is my lung capacity. The doctor told me on leaving the hospital that the echocardiogram had shown no damage to the heart even though the bacteria was in the bloodstream. That was fabulous news.

The lungs, however, were a different matter. There was damage to the lungs, and it was going to be a while before we knew how much. He cautioned me that it might take up to two years to fully recover. I promptly dismissed that, thinking that I could make something happen much faster. The stark reality of my shallow breathing and rapid loss of stamina spoke volumes otherwise.

A couple of weeks in, it dawned on me. Here was the naked truth. This incident had reduced my body to zero. I was a blank canvas, starting from scratch. I could build anything I wanted. I could build up strength and flexibility as I had previously enjoyed, but I was going to need to do the work.

Given my recent experience with miracles, I meditated and explored the possibility of creating some miraculous physical recovery.

Immediately, the impression came to me clearly and forcefully. "You had the conversations at the door. You manifested a miracle getting out of the hospital. In this case, you're going to have to do all the work."

After a bit of consideration, and looking for the gift in the answer, I saw the wisdom here. While the miracle of leaving the hospital demonstrated the power of principles and processes that would be in *The Book of Context*, the key ingredient to making all those principles produce results, is in fact, to do the work.

This was my opportunity to do the work. All the work. There was no way around it.

With that settled, I adopted a regime of regular exercise, started physical therapy and settled in for the type of system that was required in my martial arts training. It is slow; it is difficult, it requires persistence, sore muscles, and a serious commitment. However, the path is clear, and I'm on my way.

The Mental Part

I would not have expected there to be a mental recovery period. I couldn't have been more wrong. The stark reality of such an illness is that it affects every part of us.

The doctor told Joy to expect symptoms of PTSD, anxiety, continuing hallucinations and depression as part of the recovery process. She hadn't told me that at first, perhaps out of concern for worsening the regular battles I have with depression.

After a few nights, I told her I was having trouble sleeping. The first few nights she slept on the couch because she was worried her movements might keep me awake. On the contrary, being alone reminded me of the isolation and loneliness of the hospital. I lay in high anxiety unable to sleep, without knowing the reason.

I asked her to come and sleep in bed with me as we always had done. She immediately did so, and my anxiety began to subside.

Besides anxiety, I experienced some hallucinations for the first couple weeks. Not like in the hospital but disturbing nonetheless. Gradually the symptoms receded as my mind adjusted both to the reality of the physical rehabilitation and the return to normalcy for the rest of my life.

Dealing with depression is something I know well. With 45 years under my belt, the triggers, onset, and effects are as familiar as an old jacket. Knowing what to expect ahead of time allowed preparation and facilitated conversation that let me quickly gain control.

Using the routines and practices I use with my "I'm not good enough" depression, we quickly managed this new situation and reduced the noise to the level of the daily battle level of the last seven years.

I don't know if chronic MDD ever goes away. Sometimes people say it does and others say that it is permanent and only goes up and down. What I have noticed is that regular meditation has helped develop new neural pathways and habits. This lets me objectively identify symptoms and manage feelings so that it does not affect my creativity and functioning.

In my heart of hearts, I expect that with the blessing and revelation I received, as time passes and with continued diligence, the MDD will disappear entirely from my life. I believe that is possible. So far, the progress has been rapid, the mind games have stopped, and after four weeks I am back at full creative power; if only the physical part were as fast. LOL.

The Spiritual Part

This part of the game is not so much a recovery as a new benchmark for my spiritual plane and relationship with God.

I had been given information and made commitments in my conversations that radically altered everything I understood about life and increased my determination to show up in the world as an example of truths that I know.

There are two parts to this change. First is the difference in my understanding about the potential we have as children of God. Second, and more important, is a significant shift with consistency that I want to demonstrate. No more half-baked effort.

I have reflected countless times on the kindness, love, and mercy of a God who gave me so much, allowed me to return to implement it and at the same time stands ready to help me at every turn.

As the weeks have gone by, I have become increasingly focused and dedicated to the mission that I know is true and that I agreed to do. I suspect that this development will be infinite in duration. I doubt that I will ever get to a place where either God or I am completely satisfied with who I am.

After all, with God being perfect, his ability to develop us, if we are willing to walk the path, is also infinite. Just writing the sentence makes me excited and eager.

I have learned that with this commitment, I need to carry a vast blanket of forgiveness. I will attempt difficult things, and I am going to fall short. Because I came from a habit of feeling "not good enough," my tendency would naturally be to go to a place of self-criticism and negativity for not showing up all the way.

Without a doubt, self-loathing is not what God intends. For me or any of his children. Rather, it is to do everything I can, every day, to learn the lessons and do what I committed in helping each person grow and do all they can.

I can receive the gifts of failure and setbacks as opportunities for forgiveness and learning and then set out again on the adventure tomorrow.

What is gone is the baggage of doubt, the tyranny of comparing myself to imaginary standards and the endless misery of comparing my work and progress with what others are doing.

I have never experienced such glorious freedom.

I have never experienced such powerful creativity.

I have never experienced such a drive to create, to share those creations, to serve everyone in my path and to create a circle of love infinitely larger than I ever believed possible.

Chapter 20

Now – The Message and the Mission – Everywhere

I got home I have told my story.

This is what happened to me. It changed my life forever and created in me a love, a drive and a joy that is far beyond anything I have known.

The truths that I learned are powerful, eternal and apply to everyone on the earth.

<u>The Message</u>

- A divine being created every person.

- Every person has an infinite capacity.

- Every person accepted an assignment for this life.

- Every person was given gifts and talents to help accomplish this mission.

- Every person has a choice, at every moment, whether to pursue this mission.

- Every person has the means and capability of accessing their gifts and talents.

- Every person has access to divine help to perform that work.

- Every person has access to miracles and unexpected help and strength.

- Every person was designed and created to have joy and happiness.

- Every person walks their path and develops their relationship with God. We have neither the right nor the responsibility to judge those around us.

- The purpose of this life is to gain experience, pursue development and wisely exercise the gift of choice God has given us.

- God is personal and knows every one of us by name.

- God is loving, forgiving and the perfect example of how to lead with love, teach with kindness and forgive with patience.

- God is available and responds in His way to requests.

- God is at the helm and carefully walks the perfect balance between giving help and guidance and honoring our absolute right to choose.

- God has given and continues to give love, help, and guidance so we can complete our time here successfully and return to Him as triumphant stewards.

- This is the most joyous and empowering concept imaginable.

The Mission

I would not imagine that I could tell anyone else what their agreement or mission in this life might be. It has been difficult enough for me to find my own.

It has been a battle for me to make choices necessary to put off temporary enticements that have dragged me down paths of selfishness, sadness, and injury to others.

Every experience I've had is part of the tapestry of bringing me to the place where I am. Every pain, every struggle, and every bitterness has shaped me in ways that are gifts and have made me more loving, kind and sensitive to the needs of others.

Like any development process, it is slow and methodical. It takes faith, work, persistence, and trust in yourself and the processes of the Divine.

My mission is to share the experience I had at the door to eternity clearly and powerfully, everywhere I can, until I no longer draw breath.

My mission is to help those who want help finding their mission and the gifts they have were given to make it happen. It is also to help them develop the courage and commitment to bring it to life.

My mission is to be a catalyst to make things happen that otherwise would not.

My mission is to be a light and an encouragement to those who have their own pile of struggles and get lost, as I did, in darkness, self-doubt and even thoughts of self-destruction.

My mission is to love all those around me and choose every day to increase my capacity to love.

My mission is to create words and works of meaning, truth, and value.

My mission is to serve with every piece of my being and to continue on this path without regard to opposition, temporary setbacks or failings in myself or others.

A daunting task to be sure. That is as it should be. Without intense challenge and big vision, life can be small and colorless. I will succeed, and I will fail but given a big enough blanket of forgiveness and a willing and capable God in support, I know I am up to the task.

Chapter 21

Now – Your Mission, Should You Decide to Accept It – Everywhere

You too have a mission.

Perhaps you have given it deep thought, and you already know exactly what your mission is. Maybe you've written it out and made your truth and commitment statements. If so, that is wonderful and amazing. I support you with all my heart.

Most people I talk with don't have that much detail. Some have a vague feeling that they should be about something. Often, it is buried and feels inaccessible. Sometimes, they have tried a few times to understand the yearning, but have not been successful.

Sadly, sometimes life, circumstances, the opinions of others or their own previous experience have been discouraging. This leads to resignation and giving up.

Wherever you are, whatever you have done or not done, whatever has happened to you, you are called and challenged at this moment to stand up and rise to the opportunity of being the best version of yourself. What does that mean?

You have the opportunity, right here, right now, to add good to the world in your way.

You do this by finding your gifts, relying on the purpose you find in your soul, working with diligence and accessing the divine the help that is available as you seek. You can and will make a difference, make money, create lasting value and be fulfilled if you start now and never quit.

You came from the same God as I did, and your value is as high as mine. End your fear, procrastination, and self-sabotage. Instead, boldly challenge yourself to think deeply, commit fervently, dare greatly and forgive freely.

Very likely, you already know or have thoughts about just what you want to be and to do.

No more settling for what is easy and obvious. Claim your divine nature and talents and give them to the world. I can't wait to see what happens.

If I can help you or support you in your journey, then reach out. You are loved, and you are powerful.

Join me.

Epilogue

As I contemplated writing this book and baring my soul about what happened and what I agreed to do with the rest of my life, I was beset by the fears I have always had about my worth and value.

For 55+ years, I adopted the absolute belief: "I'm not good enough." That others are powerful, that others have the talents and abilities and that somehow, I was inadequate and could never really amount to much or make a difference in the world.

Those voices screamed loudly and incessantly as I thought about writing the book and particularly as I thought about boldly declaring its purpose and intention.

Gratefully, I have ignored all those voices and just told the complete and unvarnished truth as it occurred to me; before, during and after my hospital stay.

I have decided and committed to accept this assignment and return to the world to see it through. It is and will be my mission until I draw my last breath.

Ultimately, it will be your choice to decide what to do with this information. You can dismiss it as the ravings of a nutcase, or you can accept it as confirmation of deep feelings that you have always had and already knew.

Whatever you do and however you live your life, choose it boldly. Ask yourself what consequences it has on those around you. Ask yourself if you are making the best use of the gifts and talents you know you have.

Deep inside, we all know we came from a divine source. The greatest tragedy would be to ignore that voice and stamp out the feelings and yearnings that it brings.

I invite you to join me on the journey to be more and respond to the intense feelings of love and service that are innate in our divine natures.

In the book I have referred to several tools and processes that I use as part of my coaching practice or in working on volunteer assignments.

The appendix contains descriptions of these and other processes that I use in my own life and as I work with others. There is also contact information if you want to know more.

Appendix and Contact Information

For access to the resources I've talked about in this book, they are all on my website at www.kellanfluckiger.com.

- *Tightrope of Depression* is available in paperback, hardcover and digital (Kindle). This #1 best-seller is the first in a trilogy. The second book, *Down from the Gallows* is due spring 2019.

- Meditation Books – Volume I in my 5-part series is *Meditation, The Amazing Journey* Within. Four additional volumes on meditation are also available in both paperback and Kindle.

- Meditation music – there are many apps available for smartphones. I wrote a piece called *Inner Sanctum: Circles of Peace*. A sample of this music is available for free on my website.

- Information on creating effective and powerful morning rituals including Spiritual, Physical, Emotional and Mental components, and especially the powerful self-love components is part of my *Results Equation Intensive* program. More information is available at www.resultsequationsintensive.com.

- To speak with me about creating your Personal Truth and Commitment Statement (PTAC) and the other parts of that framework or to learn more about coaching and the work I do with individual and corporate clients, you will need to provide your name, email address, and phone number before booking an appointment.

- I frequently use social media as a platform to discuss everything in this book and other coaching processes that I use. Follow me on Facebook at www.facebook.com/kellan.fluckiger3

- I've created a free video series to help you get unstuck, stop procrastinating, end self-sabotage and get you moving on your way to success, prosperity, and happiness. You'll find them on my YouTube channel – The LightRope Daily Transformation for the Bold.

About the Author

Kellan Fluckiger is the author of the #1 best-selling book *Tightrope of Depression,* an in-demand speaker, and highly successful coach. Working with CEOs of companies large and small, Kellan has transformed and touched many loves over the past 30 years.

A certified master coach and former C-suite Executive, Kellan has coached everyone from Super Bowl winners to Grammy Award winners and everyone in between.

Kellan is a master at high achievement. As a motivational speaker and business coach, his journey has benefited thousands. He has written five books on meditation and provides coaching and support for creative's, entrepreneurs and leaders on their journey through struggles and victories as they discover, develop and deliver their talents to the world.

In addition to coaching, Kellan has written, recorded and produced 11 albums of original music. He's been running a successful recording studio for over 35 years. Samples of Kellan's music are available on his website at www.kellanfluckiger.com.

Born in San Francisco, Kellan now spends most of the year creating and writing in Canada with his wife, Joy, and their cats Billie and Robisco and dogs Popcorn and Cooper.